Management Accounting
Official Terminology

D0168022

The Chartered Institute of
Management Accountants
26 Chapter Street
London SW1P 4NP

First published 1982
Reprinted (with amendments) January 1984
Reprinted September 1984
Reprinted June 1987
Revised 1991, 1996

Revised in 2000 by the Chartered Institute of Management Accountants.

Reprinted April 2002

Copyright © CIMA (formerly ICMA)

ISBN 1 85971 347 5

Contents

◆
Introduction

Scope

Management accountancy covers several fields, and this terminology provides an overview of the terms relating to them. Specialist fields such as mathematics, economics, statistics, law and taxation have their own language and only brief reference can be made to them in a work of this nature. This terminology is not intended to be exhaustive but to provide an insight which should lead to further enquiry.

A number of legal definitions are included when they are important to management accounting. A much fuller selection can be seen in the *Terminology of Business and Company Law* published by the Institute.

Implementation

The terminology enables accountants to communicate more effectively, and it is suggested that they adopt the terms in accounting manuals, in common usage and in training programmes for students. Members of the Institute are expected to implement it in this way. This terminology is used by the Institute as the basis for examinations. In using it, students know that they are following the best professional practice.

Relevant definitions are included from, or based on, Statements of Standard Accounting Practice (SSAPs), Financial Reporting Standards (FRSs), Statements of Recommended Practice (SORPs), the Companies Acts, the Consortium for Advanced Manufacturers – International (CAM–I) and the British Standards Institution (BSI). In this connection SSAPs are those which were originally issued by the CCAB bodies and which have now been adopted by the Accounting Standards Board. The references to the Companies Act are to the Companies Act 1985, as modified by the Companies Act 1989.

References to FRSs and other statements are inclusive of those issued up to December 1999, including FRS 16.

No responsibility for loss occasioned to any person acting or refraining from action as a result of any material in this publication can be accepted by the authors or publishers.

International practice

The terminology is in English and applicable to most English-speaking countries. The basic definitions follow United Kingdom practice. There is a minority of synonymous terms and different usages in other territories, but a comprehensive list of such variations has not been attempted.

Reference

The terms have been classified into nine sections (Chapters 2 to 10 of this book) and are listed alphabetically within each section. For ease of reference the terms are indexed at the back of the book. Illustrations are given where it is considered that they will assist further understanding of a principle or application.

CHAPTER 1

◆

Introducing Management Accounting

Management accounting is the application of the principles of accounting and financial management to create, protect, preserve and increase value so as to deliver that value to the stakeholders of profit and not-for-profit enterprises, both public and private.

Management accounting is an integral part of management. It requires the identification, generation, presentation, interpretation and use of information relevant to:

◆ formulating business strategy;
◆ planning and controlling activities;
◆ decision-making;
◆ efficient resource usage;
◆ performance improvement and value enhancement;
◆ safeguarding tangible and intangible assets;
◆ corporate governance and internal control.

Chartered management accountants help organisations establish viable strategies and convert them into profit (in a commercial context) or into value for money (in a not-for-profit context). To achieve this they work as an integral part of multi-skilled management teams in carrying out the:

◆ formulation of policy and setting of corporate objectives (*policy determination*);
◆ formulation of strategic plans derived from corporate objectives (*strategic planning*);
◆ formulation of shorter-term opera-

tional plans (*operational planning and budgeting*);
◆ acquisition and use of finance (*treasury management*);
◆ design of systems, recording of events and transactions and management of information systems (*financial and cost accounting and systems design and management*);
◆ generation, communication and interpretation of financial and operating information for management (*management reporting*);
◆ provision of specific information on which decisions are based (*business analysis and decision support*);
◆ monitoring of outcomes against plans and other benchmarks and the initiation of responsive action for performance improvement (*financial and management control*);
◆ derivation of performance measures and benchmarks, financial and non-financial, quantitative and qualitative, for monitoring and control (*performance management*);
◆ improvement of business systems and processes through risk management and internal audit review (*performance review*).

Through these forward-looking roles and by application of their expert skills management accountants help organisations improve their performance, security, growth and competitiveness in an ever more demanding environment.

To facilitate the use of the *Official Terminology*, definitions have been classified under different headings.

Chapter 2 contains fundamental accounting concepts and terms of importance to the whole accounting discipline. Chapter 3 is devoted to cost accounting, necessary information in any business and a foundation of the management accounting function. The subsequent chapters (4, 5, 6 and 7) contain terminology related to the planning, monitoring and control cycle which comprises the management accountant's central role in the guidance and management of the organisation. The relevance of auditing, taxation and financial accounting to management accounting are recognised in Chapters 8 and 9 which centre on the stewardship function of accounting. Finally, Chapter 10 covers the broader organisational management context of management accounting with specific reference to finance and financial management.

The Terminology concludes with appendices containing listings of issued Statements of Standard Accounting Practice, Financial Reporting Standards and of acronyms commonly encountered in accounting.

For further reference:

- *BS 4335, Glossary of Terms Used in Project Network Techniques,* British Standards Institution, 1993.
- *Dictionary of Accounting and Finance,* R. Brockington, Pitman Publishing, 1993.
- *Oxford Dictionary of International Finance,* P. Moles and N. Terry, Oxford University Press, 1995.
- *Computing Terminology,* 4th edition, Ed. R.V. Franks, CIMA, 1997.
- *Terminology of Business and Company Law,* S.B. Marsh and J.B. Bailey, CIMA, 1993.

CHAPTER 2

❖

Accounting Concepts and Terms

account

A structured record of transactions in monetary terms, kept as part of an accounting system.

This may be a simple list, or entries on a debit and credit basis, maintained either manually or as a computer record. See Figure 2.1 for an illustration of the relationship of accounts.

cash account

A record of receipts and payments of cash, cheques or other forms of money transfer.

nominal account

A record of revenues and expenditures, liabilities and assets classified by their nature, e.g. sales, rent, rates, electricity, wages, share capital. These are sometimes referred to as impersonal accounts.

personal account

A record of amounts receivable from or payable to a person or an entity.

A collection of these accounts is known as a *sales/debtors ledger*, or a *purchases/creditors ledger*. The terms sales and purchases ledgers are preferred. In the USA the terms receivables ledger and payables ledger are used.

accountancy

The practice of accounting.

accountant

A member of the accountancy profession.

accounting

- ◆ the classification and recording of monetary transactions; *and*
- ◆ the presentation and interpretation of the results of those transactions in order to assess performance over a period and the financial position at a given date; and
- ◆ the monetary projection of future activities arising from alternative planned courses of action.

FIGURE 2.1 RELATIONSHIP OF ACCOUNTS

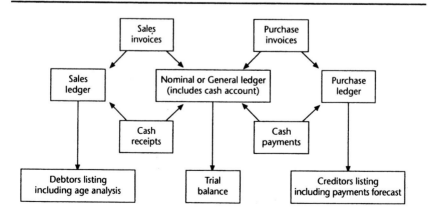

5

accounting bases

The methods used for applying fundamental accounting concepts to financial transactions and items, for the purpose of preparing financial accounts, and in particular:

◆ for determining the accounting periods in which revenue and costs should be recognised in the profit and loss account; and

◆ for determining the amounts at which material items should be stated in the balance sheet (SSAP 2).

accounting manual

A collection of accounting instructions governing the responsibilities of persons, and the procedures, forms and records relating to preparation and use of accounting data. There can be separate manuals for the constituent parts of the accounting system, e.g. budget manual, cost accounting manual.

accounting period

The time period covered by the accounting statements of an entity.

There may be different time periods for different accounting statements, e.g. management accounts may be for four- or five-week periods to coincide with a thirteen-week financial accounting period.

accounting policies

The specific accounting bases selected and consistently followed by an entity as being, in the opinion of the management, appropriate to its circumstances and best suited to present fairly its results and financial position (SSAP 2 and Companies Act). For example, from the various possible methods of depreciation, the accounting policy may be to use straight-line depreciation.

accounting standard

Authoritative statement of how particular types of transaction and other events should be reflected in financial statements. Compliance with accounting standards will normally be necessary for financial statements to give a true and fair view (ASB).

Accounting Standards Board (ASB)

A UK standard-setting body established on 1 August 1990 to develop, issue and withdraw accounting standards. Its aims are 'to establish and improve standards of financial accounting and reporting, for the benefit of users, preparers and auditors of financial information' (ASB).

accounting system

The series of tasks and records of an entity by which the transactions are processed as a means of maintaining financial records. Such systems identify, assemble, analyse, calculate, classify, record, summarise and report transactions and other events (SAS 300).

agency theory

Hypothesis that attempts to explain elements of organisational behaviour through an understanding of the relationships between principals (such as shareholders) and agents (such as company managers and accountants). A conflict may exist between the actions undertaken by agents in furtherance of their own self-interest, and those required to promote the interests of the principals. Within the hierarchy of firms, the same goal incongruence may arise when divisional managers promote their own self-interest over those of other divisions and of the company generally.

analytical review

The examination of ratios, trends and changes in balances from one period to the next, to obtain a broad understanding of the financial position and results of operations; and to identify any items requiring further investigation.

audit

A systematic examination of the activities and status of an entity, based primarily on investigation and analysis of its systems, controls and records.

compliance audit

An audit of specific activities in order to determine whether performance is in conformity with a predetermined contractual, regulatory or statutory requirement.

cost audit

The verification of cost records and accounts and a check on adherence to prescribed cost accounting procedures and their continuing relevance.

environmental audit

A systematic, documented, periodic and objective evaluation of how well an organisation, its management and equipment are performing, with the aim of helping to safeguard the environment by:

◆ facilitating management control of environmental practices;

◆ assessing compliance with company policies and external regulations.

external audit

A periodic examination of the books of account and records of an entity carried out by an independent third party (the auditor) to ensure that they have been properly maintained, are accurate and comply with established concepts, principles, accounting standards, legal requirements and give a true and fair view of the financial state of the entity.

internal audit

An independent appraisal function established within an organisation to examine and evaluate its activities as a service to the organisation. The objective of internal auditing is to assist members of the organisation in the effective discharge of their responsibilities. To this end, internal auditing furnishes them with analyses, appraisals, recommendations, counsel and information concerning the activities reviewed (Institute of Internal Auditors–UK).

management audit

An objective and independent appraisal of the effectiveness of managers and the corporate structure in the achievement of entity objectives and policies. Its aim is to identify existing and potential management weaknesses and to recommend ways to rectify them.

post-completion audit

An objective and independent appraisal of the measure of success of a capital expenditure project in progressing the business as planned. The appraisal should cover the implementation of the project from authorisation to commissioning and its technical and commercial performance after commissioning. The information provided is also used by management as feedback which aids the implementation and control of future projects.

value for money audit

An investigation into whether proper arrangements have been made for securing economy, efficiency and effectiveness in the use of resources.

audit committee

A formally constituted sub-committee of the main board which should normally meet at least twice a year. Membership of the committee should comprise at least three directors, all non-executive. A majority of the committee members should be independent of the company. The primary function of the audit committee is to assist the board to fulfil its stewardship responsibilities by reviewing the systems of internal control, the external audit process, the work of internal audit and the financial information which is provided to shareholders.

audit trail

The linked chain of evidence which connects an item in the accounts with the source document which verifies its validity.

Auditing Practices Board (APB)

A body formed in 1991 by an agreement between the six members of the *Consultative Committee of Accountancy Bodies*, to be responsible for developing and issuing professional standards for auditors in the United Kingdom and the Republic of Ireland.

balance (on an account)

The difference between the totals of the debit and credit entries in an account.

behavioural implications

The ways in which humans affect, and are affected by, the creation, existence and use of accounting information.

bookkeeping

Recording of monetary transactions, appropriately classified, in the financial records of an entity, either by manual means, or otherwise. *See* double entry bookkeeping.

call off

System whereby inventory is held at the customer's premises, to be invoiced only on use.

capital gain (loss)

The extent by which the net realised value of a capital asset exceeds (or in the case of a capital loss is less than) the cost of acquisition plus additional improvements, less depreciation charges where applicable.

It can also arise from the exchange of such an asset for another of a different type. The term can have other interpretations for tax purposes.

capital maintenance

The principle that profit is only recorded after capital has been maintained intact. There are two bases on which capital can be defined, financial and physical.

financial

The concept that profit is earned only if the financial (or money) amount of the net assets at the end of the period exceeds the financial (or money) amount of net assets at the beginning of the period, after excluding any distributions to, and contributions from, owners during the period *(International Accounting Standards Committee Framework)*. *See* current purchasing power accounting.

physical

The concept that profit is earned only if the physical productive capacity (or operating capability) of the enterprise (or the resources or funds needed to achieve that capacity) at the end of the period exceeds the physical productive capacity at the beginning of the period, after excluding any distributions to, and contributions from, owners during the period *(International Accounting Standards Committee Framework). See* current cost accounting.

capital surplus
Assets remaining in the liquidation of a company after all costs and liabilities have been met. It is distributed among shareholders in accordance with their rights under the articles of association.

cash
Cash in hand and deposits repayable on demand with any bank or other financial institution. Cash includes cash in hand and deposits denominated in foreign currencies (FRS 1).

chart of accounts
A comprehensive and systematically arranged list of the named and numbered accounts applicable to an enterprise. *See* Figure 2.2.

classification
The arrangement of items in logical groups having regard to their nature (subjective classification) or purpose (objective classification). *See* code.

FIGURE 2.2 EXTRACT FROM CHART OF ACCOUNTS

Code	Account descriptor
1	Assets
2	Liabilities
3	Equity
4	Expenses
5	Revenue
11	Fixed assets
12	Current assets
111	Land
112	Buildings
113	Plant
114	Motor vehicles

code
A system of symbols designed to be applied to a classified set of items to give a brief, accurate reference, facilitating entry, collation and analysis.

For example, in costing systems, composite symbols are commonly used. In the composite symbol 211.392 the first three digits might indicate the nature of the expenditure *(subjective classification)*, and the last three digits might indicate the cost centre or cost unit to be charged *(objective classification)*.

commitment accounting
A method of accounting which recognises expenditure as soon as it is contracted.

commodity pricing
Pricing a product or service on the basis that it is undifferentiated from all competitive offerings, and cannot therefore command any price premium above the base market price.

concepts
Principles underpinning the preparation of accounting information. *See* fundamental accounting concepts and fundamental management accounting concepts.

fundamental accounting concepts
Broad basic assumptions which underlie the periodic financial accounts of business enterprises (SSAP 2).

accruals concept
The principle that revenue and costs are recognised as they are earned or incurred, are matched with one another, and are dealt with in the profit and loss account of the period to which they relate, irrespective of the period of receipt or payment. Where a conflict arises, this concept is subservient to the prudence concept (SSAP 2). Also called the matching concept.

consistency concept
The principle that there is unifor-

mity of accounting treatment of like items within each accounting period and from one period to the next (SSAP 2).

going concern concept
The assumption that the entity will continue in operational existence for the foreseeable future (SSAP 2). The assumption that a particular entity is a going concern can now be operationally tested by statistical models for firms operating in well-defined business areas. *See* Z score (Chapter 10).

prudence concept
The principle that revenue and profits are not anticipated, but are included in the profit and loss account only when realised in the form either of cash or of other assets, the ultimate cash realisation of which can be assessed with reasonable certainty; provision is made for all known liabilities (expenses and losses) whether the amount of these is known with certainty or is a best estimate in the light of the information available (SSAP 2). This may also be termed *conservatism*

separate valuation
In determining the aggregate amount of any item the amount of each individual asset or liability that falls to be taken into account shall be determined separately (1985 Companies Act).

fundamental management accounting concepts
Fundamental principles for the preparation of management accounting information (International Management Accounting Practice Statement No.1 of the Financial and Management Accounting Committee of IFAC).

accountability concept
Management accounting presents information measuring the achievement of the objectives of an organisation and appraising the conduct of its internal affairs in that process. In order that further action can be taken, based on this information, it is necessary at all times to identify the responsibilities and key results of individuals within the organisation.

controllability concept
Management accounting identifies the elements or activities which management can or cannot influence, and seeks to assess risk and sensitivity factors. This facilitates the proper monitoring, analysis, comparison and interpretation of information which can be used constructively in the control, evaluation and corrective functions of management.

interdependency concept
Management accounting, in recognition of the increasing complexity of business, must access both external and internal information sources from interactive functions such as marketing, production, personnel, procurement and finance. This assists in ensuring that the information is adequately balanced.

relevancy concept
Management accounting must ensure that flexibility is maintained in assembling and interpreting information. This facilitates the exploration and presentation, in a clear, understandable and timely manner, of as many alternatives as are necessary for impartial and confident decisions to be taken.
The process is essentially forward-looking and dynamic. Therefore, the information must

satisfy the criteria of being applicable and appropriate.

reliability concept
Management accounting information must be of such quality that confidence can be placed in it. Its reliability to the user is dependent on its source, integrity and comprehensiveness.

other concepts

business entity concept
The concept that financial accounting information relates only to the activities of the business entity and not to the activities of its owner(s).

cost (at cost) concept
The practice of valuing assets with reference to their acquisition cost.

materiality concept
Information is material if its omission or misstatement could influence the economic decisions of users taken on the basis of the financial statements. Materiality depends on the size of the item or error judged in the particular circumstances of its omission or misstatement. Thus, materiality provides a threshold or cut-off point rather than being a primary qualitative characteristic that information must have if it is to be useful (ASB Statement of Principles).

periodicity concept
The requirement to produce financial statements at set time intervals. This requirement is embodied, in the case of UK corporations, in the Companies Acts.

realisation concept
The principle that increases in value should only be recognised on realisation of assets by arm's-length sale to an independent purchaser.

substance over form concept
Where a conflict exists, the structuring of reports to give precedence to the representation of financial reality over strict adherence to the requirements of the legal reporting structure.

consolidation accounting
The process of adjusting and combining financial information from the individual financial statements of a parent undertaking and its subsidiary undertakings to prepare consolidated financial statements that present financial information for the group as a single economic entity (FRS 2).

acquisition accounting
A method of accounting which regards the business combination as the acquisition of one company by another: the identifiable assets and liabilities of the company acquired are included in the consolidated balance sheet at their fair value at the date of acquisition, and its results included in the profit and loss account from the date of acquisition. The difference between the fair value of the consideration given and the fair values of the net assets of the entity acquired is accounted for as goodwill (FRS 6).

merger accounting
A method of accounting which treats two or more parties as combining on an equal footing. It is normally applied without any restatement of net assets to fair value, and includes the results of each for the whole of the accounting period. Correspondingly, it does not reflect the issue of shares as an application of resources at fair value. The difference that arises on consolidation does not represent goodwill but is deducted from, or added to, reserves (FRS 6).

contingency theory
Hypothesis that there can be no

universally applicable best practice in the design of organisational units or of control systems such as management accounting systems. The efficient design and functioning of such systems is dependent on an awareness by the system designer of the specific environmental factors which influence their operation, such as the organisational structure, technology base and market situation.

continuing operations
See discontinued operations.

contra
A bookkeeping term meaning against, or on the opposite side. It is used where debits are matched with related credits, in the same or a different account. (A common example is where a supplier is also a customer.)

control
The ability to direct the financial and operating policies of an entity with a view to gaining economic benefits from its activities (FRS 8). *See* cost control, internal control, internal control system, internal financial control, management control.

control environment
The overall attitude, awareness and actions of directors and management regarding internal controls and their importance to the entity. The control environment encompasses the management style, and corporate culture and values shared by all employees. It provides a background against which the various other controls are operated (SAS 300).

control procedures
Those policies and procedures in addition to the control environment which are established to achieve the entity's specific objectives. They include in particular procedures designed to prevent or to detect and correct errors (SAS 300).

corporate social accounting
The reporting of the social and environmental impact of an entity's activities upon those who are directly associated with the entity (employees, customers, suppliers, etc.) or those who are in any way affected by the activities of the entity, as well as an assessment of the cost of compliance with relevant regulations in this area.

cost
(as a noun). The amount of expenditure (actual or notional) incurred on, or attributable to, a specified thing or activity.
(as a verb). To ascertain the cost of a specified thing or activity.
The word cost can rarely stand alone and should be qualified as to its nature and limitations.

cost accounting
The establishment of budgets, standard costs and actual costs of operations, processes, activities or products; and the analysis of variances, profitability or the social use of funds. The use of the term 'costing' is not recommended except with a qualifying adjective, e.g. standard costing.

creative accounting
A form of accounting which, while complying with all regulations, nevertheless gives a biased impression (generally favourable) of the company's performance. *See* window-dressing.

credit scoring
The assessment of the creditworthiness of an individual or company by rating numerically a number of

both financial and non-financial aspects of the target's present position and previous performance.

crystallisation

The process whereby a floating charge relating to company assets becomes fixed to the assets to which it relates.

current cost accounting (CCA)

A method of accounting in which profit is defined as 'the surplus after allowing for price changes on the funds needed to continue the existing business and to maintain its operating capability, whether financed by shares or borrowing'. A CCA balance sheet shows the effect of physical capital maintenance.

current purchasing power accounting (CPP)

A method of accounting in which the values of non-monetary items in the historical cost accounts are adjusted, using a general price index, so that the resulting profit allows for the maintenance of the purchasing power of the shareholders' interest in the organisation. A CPP balance sheet shows the effect of financial capital maintenance.

discontinued operations

Operations of the reporting entity that are sold or terminated and that satisfy all the following conditions:

(a) The sale or termination is completed either in the period or before the earlier of three months after the commencement of the subsequent period and the date on which the financial statements are approved.

(b) If a termination, the former activities have ceased permanently.

(c) The sale or termination has a material effect on the nature and focus of the reporting

entity's operations, and represents a material reduction in its operating facilities resulting either from its withdrawal from a particular market (whether class of business or geographical) or from a material reduction in turnover in the reporting entity's continuing markets.

(d) The assets, liabilities, results of operations and activities are clearly distinguishable physically, operationally and for financial reporting purposes.

Operations not satisfying all these conditions are classified as *continuing* (FRS 3).

dominant influence

Influence that can be exercised to achieve the operating and financial policies designed by the holder of the influence, notwithstanding the rights or influence of any other party (FRS 2).

double entry bookkeeping/ accounting

The most commonly used system of bookkeeping based on the principle that every financial transaction involves the simultaneous receiving and giving of value, and is therefore recorded twice.

e-commerce

Trading on the internet.

equity method of accounting

A method of accounting for an investment that brings into the consolidated profit and loss account the investor's share of the investment undertaking's results and that records the investment in the consolidated balance sheet at the investor's share of the investment undertaking's net assets including any goodwill arising to the extent that it has not previously been written off (FRS 2).

ex gratia

As an act of favour, without obligation. There is no obligation to make an ex gratia payment.

fair value

The amount for which an asset (or liability) could be exchanged in an arm's-length transaction between informed and willing parties, other than in a forced or liquidation sale (FRS 7).

financial accounting

The classification and recording of the monetary transactions of an entity in accordance with established concepts, principles, accounting standards and legal requirements and their presentation, by means of profit and loss accounts, balance sheets and cash flow statements, during and at the end of an accounting period.

financial management

The management of all the processes associated with the efficient acquisition and deployment of both short- and long-term financial resources.

Financial Reporting Council

The UK body responsible for:

(i) guiding the standard setting body (ASB) on work programmes and issues of public concern

(ii) seeing that work on accounting standards is properly financed

(iii) acting as a proactive public influence for securing good accounting practice (ASB).

Financial Reporting Review Panel

A UK review panel established to examine contentious departures, by large companies, from accounting standards.

Financial Reporting Standard (FRS)

A UK accounting standard issued from 1 August 1990, when the Accounting Standards Board (ASB) succeeded the Accounting Standards Committee (ASC).

forensic accounting

The use of accounting records and documents in order to determine the legality or otherwise of past activities.

fund accounting

The preparation of financial statements for an entity which is a fund.

Such statements are usually on a cash basis and are most commonly found in the public sector, e.g. Consolidated Fund and National Loans Fund.

historical cost

The original acquisition cost of an asset, unadjusted for subsequent price level or value changes.

historical cost accounting

A system of accounting in which all values are based on the historical costs incurred. This is the basis prescribed in the Companies Act for published accounts. (*Note*: The Companies Act also contains Alternative Accounting Rules which enable certain assets to be stated at revalued amounts.)

human resource accounting

The identification, recording and reporting of the investment in, and return from the employment of, the personnel of an organisation.

imprest system

A method of controlling cash or stock: when the cash or stock has been reduced by disbursements or issues it is restored to its original level.

incomplete records

An accounting system which is not double-entry bookkeeping.

Various degrees of incompleteness can occur, e.g. *single-entry bookkeeping*, in which usually only a cash book is maintained.

insolvency
The inability of a company, partnership or individual to pay creditors' debts in full after realisation of all the assets of the business.

integrated accounts
A set of accounting records which provides both financial and cost accounts using a common input of data for all accounting purposes.

intellectual capital
Knowledge which can be used to create value. Intellectual capital includes (i) *human resources*: the collective skills, experience and knowledge of employees; (ii) *intellectual assets*: knowledge which is defined and codified such as a drawing, computer program or collection of data; and (iii) *intellectual property*: intellectual assets which can be legally protected, such as patents and copyrights.

interlocking accounts/non-integrated accounts
A system in which the cost accounts are distinct from the financial accounts, the two sets of accounts being kept continuously in agreement by the use of control accounts or reconciled by other means.

internal check
The procedures designed to provide assurance that:
◆ everything which should be recorded has been recorded;
◆ errors or irregularities are identified;
◆ assets and liabilities exist and are correctly recorded.

internal control
The whole system of controls, financial and otherwise, established in order to provide reasonable assurance of:
(a) effective and efficient operation;
(b) internal financial control;

(c) compliance with laws and regulations.
(Cadbury Report)

internal financial control
The internal controls established in order to provide reasonable assurance of:
(a) the safeguarding of assets against unauthorised use or disposition;
(b) the maintenance of proper accounting records and the reliability of financial information used within the business or for publication.
(Cadbury Report)

International Accounting Standards Committee (IASC)
Committee supported by many national accounting bodies worldwide, whose objects are: (a) to facilitate and publish in the public interest, accounting standards to be observed in the presentation of financial statements, and to promote their worldwide acceptance and observance, and (b) to work generally for the improvement of harmonisation of regulations, accounting standards and procedures relating to the presentation of financial statements (IASC).

ledger
A collection of accounts, or book of accounts, e.g. credit sales information is recorded, by debtor, in the *sales ledger*.

management accounting
The application of the principles of accounting and financial management to create, protect, preserve and increase value so as to deliver that value to the stakeholders of profit and not-for-profit enterprises, both public and private. Management accounting is an integral part of management, requiring the identification, generation, presentation,

interpretation and use of information relevant to:

◆ formulating business strategy;
◆ planning and controlling activities;
◆ decision-making;
◆ efficient resource usage;
◆ performance improvement and value enhancement;
◆ safeguarding tangible and intangible assets;
◆ corporate governance and internal control.

net realisable value (NRV)
The amount for which an asset could be disposed, less any direct selling costs (FRS10).

off balance sheet finance
The funding of operations in such a way that the relevant assets and liabilities are not disclosed in the balance sheet of the company concerned. *See* concept, substance over form.

ordinary activities
Any activities which are undertaken by a reporting entity as part of its business and such related activities in which the reporting entity engages in furtherance of, incidental to, or arising from, these activities. Ordinary activities include the effects on the reporting entity of any event in the various environments in which it operates, including the political, regulatory, economic and geographical environments, irrespective of the frequency or unusual nature of the events (FRS 3).

performance measurement
The process of assessing the proficiency with which a reporting entity succeeds, by the economic acquisition of resources and their efficient and effective deployment, in achieving its objectives. Performance measures may be based on

non-financial as well as on financial information.

pricing
The determination of a selling price for the product or service produced. A number of methodologies may be used, including:

competitive pricing
Setting a price by reference to the prices of competitive products.

cost plus pricing
The determination of price by adding a mark-up, which may incorporate a desired return on investment, to a measure of the cost of the product/service.

dual pricing
A form of transfer pricing in which the two parties to a common transaction use different prices.

historical pricing
Basing current prices on prior period prices, perhaps uplifted by a factor such as inflation.

market based pricing
Setting a price based on the value of the product in the perception of the customer. Also known as perceived value pricing.

penetration pricing
Setting a low selling price in order to gain market share.

predatory pricing
Setting a low selling price in order to damage competitors. This may involve dumping, which is selling a product in a foreign market at below cost, or below the domestic market price (subject to adjustments for taxation differences, transportation costs, specification differences etc.).

premium pricing
The achievement of a price above the commodity level, due to a measure of product or service differentiation.

price skimming
Setting a high price in order to maximise short-term profitability, often on the introduction of a novel product.

range pricing
The pricing of individual products such that their prices fit logically within a range of connected products offered by one supplier, and differentiated by a factor such as weight of pack or number of product attributes offered.

selective pricing
Setting different prices for the same product or service in different markets. This practice can be broken down as follows:
- ◆ *category pricing*
  Cosmetically modifying a product such that the variations allow it to sell in a number of price categories, as where a range of 'brands' are based on a common product.
- ◆ *customer group pricing*
  Modifying the price of a product or service so that different groups of consumers pay different prices.
- ◆ *peak pricing*
  Setting a price which varies according to level of demand.
- ◆ *service level pricing*
  Setting a price based on the particular level of service chosen from a range.

time and material pricing
A form of cost plus pricing in which price is determined by reference to the cost of the labour and material inputs to the product/service

product bundling
A form of discounting in which a group of related products is sold at a price which is lower that that obtainable by the consumer were the products to be purchased separately.

profit margin
Sales less cost of sales, expressed either as a value or as a percentage of sales value. The profit margin may be calculated at different stages, hence the terms *gross* and *net profit margin*. The level of profit reported is also influenced by the extent of the application of accounting conventions, and by the method of product costing used, e.g. marginal or absorption costing.

qualitative factors
Factors which are relevant to a decision, but which are not expressed numerically.

quantitative factors
Factors which are relevant to a decision and which are expressed numerically.

receivership
Under the control of a receiver, who is appointed by secured creditors or by the court to take control of company property. The most usual reason for the appointment of a receiver is the failure of a company to pay principal sums or interest due to debenture holders whose debt is secured by fixed or floating charges over the assets of the company.

recognition
The process of incorporating an item into the primary financial statements under the appropriate heading. It involves depiction of the item in words and by a monetary amount and inclusion of that amount in the statement totals (FRS 5).

regulatory framework
The set of legal and professional requirements with which the financial statements of a company must comply. Company reporting is

influenced by the requirements of law, of the accountancy profession and of the stock exchange (for listed companies).

return on sales
See profit margin.

services
Value-creating activities which in themselves do not involve the supply of physical product. Service provision may be subdivided into: (i) *Pure services* where there is no physical product, such as consultancy, (ii) *services with a product attached*, such as the design and installation of a computer network, and (iii) *products with services attached*, such as the purchase of a computer with a maintenance contract.

short-termism
Bias towards paying particular attention to short-term performance, with a corresponding relative disregard to the long run.

social cost
Tangible and intangible costs and losses sustained by third parties or the general public as a result of economic activity, e.g. pollution by industrial effluent.

social responsibility accounting
The identification, measurement and reporting of the social costs and benefits resulting from economic activities.

stakeholders
Groups or individuals having a legitimate interest in the activities of an organisation, generally comprising customers, employees, the community, shareholders, suppliers and lenders.

Statement of Auditing Standards (SAS)
An auditing standard, issued by the Auditing Practices Board (APB), containing prescriptions as to the basic principles and practices which members of the UK accountancy bodies are expected to follow in the course of an audit.

Statement of Standard Accounting Practice (SSAP)
An accounting standard issued by the Accounting Standards Committee (ASC). See Financial Reporting Standard.

stewardship
The responsibility of agents to act in the best interests of their principals, by keeping adequate records of transactions and by acting so as to maintain or increase both the capital and income of the principal.

teeming and lading
A fraud based on a continuous cycle of stealing and later replacing assets (generally cash), each theft being used in part, or in full, to repay a previous theft in order to avoid detection.

timing difference
A difference between the balances held on related accounts which is caused by differences in the timing of the input of common transactions, e.g. a direct debit will appear on the bank statement before it is entered into the bank account. Knowledge of the timing difference allows the balances on the two accounts to be reconciled, however.

treasury management
The corporate handling of all financial matters, the generation of external and internal funds for business, the management of currencies and cash flows, and the complex strategies, policies and procedures of corporate finance (Association of Corporate Treasurers). See Figure 2.3.

uniform accounting
A system by which different organi-

FIGURE 2.3 RELATIONSHIP OF THE TREASURY AND CONTROL FUNCTIONS

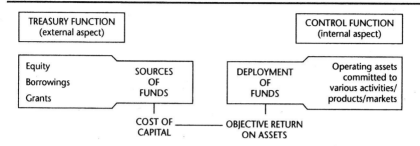

sations in the same industry adopt common concepts, principles and assumptions in order to facilitate interfirm comparison or a system of classifying financial accounts in a similar manner within defined business sectors of a national economy, to ensure comparability.

Urgent Issues Task Force (UITF)
An organisation whose aim is to assist the ASB in areas where unsatisfactory or conflicting interpretations of an accounting standard have developed, or seem likely to develop.

user groups
Different interest groups who may make use of publicly available financial statements. Lenders, employees, investors and competitors may be classed as separate user groups.

value added
Sales value less the cost of purchased materials and services. This represents the worth of an alteration in form, location or availability of a product or service.

window-dressing
A creative accounting practice in which changes in short-term funding have the effect of disguising or improving the reported liquidity position of the reporting organisation.

CHAPTER 3

❖

Cost Ascertainment and Cost Management

abnormal loss/gain

Any losses which exceed the normal loss allowance (abnormal loss) or reduction in the volume of process loss below that set by the normal loss allowance (abnormal gain). Abnormal losses and gains are generally costed as though they were completed products.

absorbed overhead

Overhead attached to products or services by means of absorption rates. *Under- or over-absorbed overhead.* The difference between overhead incurred and overhead absorbed, using an estimated rate, in a given period. In a standard costing system, it is the sum of variable production overhead total variance and fixed production overhead total variance. Under- or over-absorbed may also be expressed as under- or over-recovered. *See* Figure 3.4.

absorption rate

See overhead absorption rate.

activity-based costing (ABC)

An approach to the costing and monitoring of activities which involves tracing resource consumption and costing final outputs. Resources are assigned to activities and activities to cost objects based on consumption estimates. The latter utilise cost drivers to attach activity costs to outputs. *See* Figure 3.2.

activity-based management (ABM)

System of management which uses activity-based cost information for a variety of purposes including cost reduction, cost modelling and customer profitability analysis.

activity cost pool

A grouping of all cost elements associated with an activity (CAM–I).

activity driver

A measure of the frequency and intensity of the demands placed on activities by cost objects. For example, the number of customer orders measures the consumption of order entry activities by each customer (CAM–I).

activity driver analysis

The identification and evaluation of the activity drivers used to trace the cost of activities to cost objects. It may also involve selecting activity drivers with potential to contribute to the cost management function with particular reference to cost reduction.

allocate

To assign a whole item of cost, or of revenue, to a single cost unit, centre, account or time period. *See* Figure 3.4.

apportion

To spread revenues or costs over two or more cost units, centres, accounts or time periods. This may also be referred to as 'indirect allocation'. *See* Figure 3.4.

available hours

The number of hours for which a worker or machine is available to work.

In a simple case for a worker this could be as follows for a four-week period:

	Hours
Numbers of contractual hours	140
Overtime hours	20
Absence: Public holidays 7	
Annual holidays 28	
Certified sickness 14	
Other absence 1	(50)
Available hours	110

avoidable costs

The specific costs of an activity or sector of a business which would be avoided if that activity or sector did not exist.

backflush costing

A method of costing, associated with a JIT production system, which applies cost to the output of a process. Costs do not mirror the flow of products through the production process, but are attached to output produced (finished goods stock and cost of sales), on the assumption that such backflushed costs are a realistic measure of the actual costs incurred.

balanced scorecard approach

An approach to the provision of information to management to assist strategic policy formulation and achievement. It emphasises the need to provide the user with a set of information which addresses all relevant areas of performance in an objective and unbiased fashion. The information provided may include both financial and non-financial elements, and cover areas such as profitability, customer satisfaction, internal efficiency and innovation.

basis of apportionment

A physical or financial unit used to apportion costs equitably to cost centres.

batch

A group of similar articles which maintains its identity throughout one or more stages of production and is treated as a cost unit.

batch-level activities

Activities which vary directly with the number of batches of output produced, and which are independent of the number of units within a batch. Set up costs are batch-level activities. *See* hierarchy of activities.

benchmarking

The establishment, through data gathering, of targets and comparators, through whose use relative levels of performance (and particularly areas of underperformance) can be identified. By the adoption of identified best practices it is hoped that performance will improve. Types of benchmarking include:

♦ *Internal benchmarking*, a method of comparing one operating unit or function with another within the same industry.

♦ *Functional benchmarking*, in which internal functions are compared with those of the best external practitioners of those functions, regardless of the industry they are in (also known as operational benchmarking or generic benchmarking).

♦ *Competitive benchmarking*, in which information is gathered about direct competitors, through techniques such as reverse engineering.

♦ *Strategic benchmarking*, a type of competitive benchmarking aimed at strategic action and organisational change.

bill of materials

A detailed specification, for each product produced, of the subassemblies, components and materials required, distinguishing between those items which are purchased externally and those which are manufactured in-house.

FIGURE 3.1 ELEMENTS OF A PRODUCT COSTING SYSTEM (See page 38)

Overall Control System: Budgetary Control				
Product costing system	Specific orders		Continuous operations	
Costing method	Job costing	Batch costing Contract costing	Continuous operation/ process costing	Service/ function costing
Treatment of fixed production overhead	Absorption or marginal			
Method of cost control	Standard or actual			

FIGURE 3.2 THE FRAMEWORK OF ACTIVITY-BASED COSTING

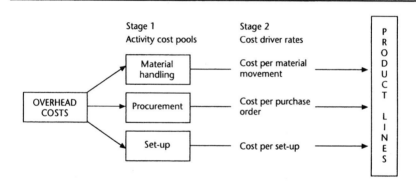

bin card
A record of receipts, issues and balances of the quantity of an item of stock handled by a store.

bottleneck
An activity within an organisation which has a lower capacity than preceding or subsequent activities, thereby limiting throughput. Bottlenecks are often the cause of a build-up of work in progress and of idle time. *See* theory of constraints.

buffer stock
A stock of materials, or of work in progress, maintained in order to protect user departments from the effect of possible interruptions to supply.

business process re-engineering
The selection of areas of business activity in which repeatable and repeated sets of activities are undertaken, and the development of improved understanding of how they operate and of the scope for radical redesign with a view to creating and delivering better customer value.

by-product
Output of some value produced incidentally in manufacturing something else (main product). *See* joint products.

FIGURE 3.3 CAUSE AND EFFECT/FISHBONE DIAGRAM

(a) Identification of the possible causes of paint blemishes

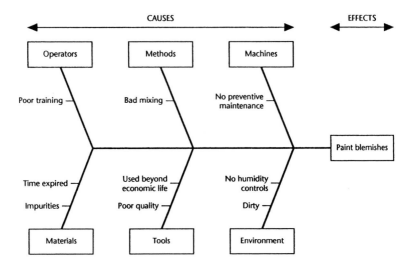

(b) Identification of possible ways to improve the quality of paintwork

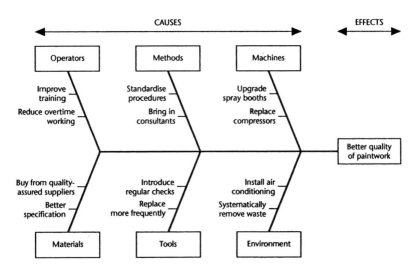

FIGURE 3.4 COST ALLOCATION, APPORTIONMENT AND OVERHEAD ABSORPTION

	FACTORY TOTAL	PRODUCTION COST CENTRES		SERVICE COST CENTRES			
		Machine Shop	Assembly Department	Engineering Services	Stores	Factory Admin	Quality Control
	£	£ DIRECT COST £		£	£	£	£
ATTRIBUTION OF BUDGETED PAYROLL COST							
DIRECT WAGES COST – time worked on products allocated to products	X	X	X				
INDIRECT WAGES COST AND SALARIES							
Direct workers' time not working on products	X	X	X				
Sickness, holiday, NI and pension costs	X	X	X				
Indirect workers' wages and employment costs	X	X	X	X	X	X	X
Supervision salaries & employment costs	X	X	X				
Engineering salaries & employment costs	X			X			
Quality control salaries & employment costs	X						X
Storekeepers' salaries & employment costs	X				X		
Other salaries	X					X	
TOTAL OVERHEAD PAYROLL COST	X	X	X	X	X	X	X
Other allocated overhead	X	X	X	X	X	X	X
Apportioned costs, e.g. building service costs	X	X	X	X	X	X	X
TOTAL BUDGETED PRODUCTION OVERHEAD	X	X	X	X	X	X	X
Re-apportionment of service cost centre costs		X	X				

COST ALLOCATION

COST APPORTIONMENT

OVERHEAD ABSORPTION

	Product cost per unit	
Direct material cost allocated	X	£/machine hour £/direct labour hour (Absorption rates) £/unit
Direct wages cost allocated	X	
Production overhead		
– machine shop	X	
– assembly	X	
– quality control	X	
Production cost per unit	X	

cause and effect diagram
A diagram that aids the generation and sorting of the potential causes of variations in an activity or process. Also known as a fishbone diagram. *See* Figure 3.3

centre
Department, area or function to which costs and/or revenues are charged. *See* Figure 3.4

budget centre
A centre for which an individual budget is drawn up.

contribution centre
A profit centre in which marginal or direct costs are matched against revenue.

cost centre
A production or service location, function, activity or item of equipment for which costs are accumulated. *See* Figure 3.4.

investment centre
A profit centre with additional responsibilities for capital investment and possibly for financing,

and whose performance is measured by its return on investment.

profit centre

A part of a business accountable for both costs and revenues.

responsibility centre

A department or organisational function whose performance is the direct responsibility of a specific manager.

revenue centre

A centre devoted to raising revenue with no responsibility for costs, e.g. a sales centre. Often used in a not-for-profit organisation.

service cost centre

A cost centre providing services to other cost centres. When the output of an organisation is a service, rather than goods, an alternative name is normally used, e.g. support cost centre or utility cost centre. *See* Figure 3.4.

clock card

A document on which is recorded the starting and finishing time of an employee, e.g. by insertion into a time-recording device, for ascertaining total actual attendance time.

Where an employee also clocks on and off different jobs within total attendance time, such cards are referred to as job cards.

commitment accounting

A method of accounting which recognises expenditure as soon as it is contracted. Support systems such as purchase order processing may be required for implementation.

committed costs

Costs arising from prior decisions, which cannot, in the short run, be changed. Committed cost incurrence often stems from strategic decisions concerning capacity, with resulting expenditure on plant and

FIGURE 3.5 COMPARISON, OVER THE LIFE OF A PROJECT, OF THE DIFFERENCES BETWEEN COST COMMITMENT AND COST INCURRENCE

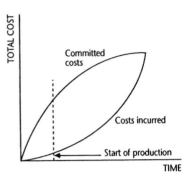

By the start of the production period, most of the costs which will be incurred have already been designed into the product and the selected production technology, and are, once production starts, only marginally susceptible to change.

facilities. Initial control of committed costs at the decision point is through investment appraisal techniques. *See* commitment accounting. *See* Figure 3.5.

common cost

Cost relating to more than one product or service.

competitor analysis

The identification and quantification of the relative strengths and weaknesses (compared with competitors or potential competitors), which could be of significance in the development of a successful competitive strategy.

consignment stock

Stock held by one party (the 'dealer') but legally owned by another (the 'manufacturer'), on terms that give the dealer the right to sell the stock in the normal course of its business or, at its option, to return it unsold to the legal owner (FRSSE).

constraint

An activity, resource or policy that limits the ability to achieve objectives. Constraints are commonly used in mathematical programming to describe a restriction which forms part of the boundary for the range of solutions to a problem, and which define the area within which the solution must lie. *See* Figure 3.11.

contract cost

Aggregated costs of a single contract; usually applies to major long-term contracts rather than short-term jobs.

contribution

Sales value less variable cost of sales. Contribution may be expressed as total contribution, contribution per unit or as a percentage of sales. *See* Figure 3.6.

controllable cost

A cost which can be influenced by its budget holder.

conversion cost

Cost of converting material into finished products, i.e. direct labour, direct expense and production overhead.

cost account

A record of revenue and/or expenditure of a cost centre or cost unit.

cost behaviour

The variability of input costs with activity undertaken. A number of cost behaviour patterns are possible, ranging from variable costs whose cost level varies directly with the level of activity, to fixed costs, where changes in output have no effect upon the cost level. *See* Figures 3.7 and 3.8.

cost-benefit analysis

A comparison between the cost of the resources used, plus any other costs imposed by an activity (e.g.

pollution, environmental damage) and the value of the financial and non-financial benefits derived.

cost classification

The arrangement of elements of cost into logical groups with respect to their nature (fixed, variable, value adding etc.), function (production, selling etc.) or use in the business of the entity.

cost control

The process which ensures that actual costs do not exceed acceptable limits.

cost driver

Any factor which causes a change in the cost of an activity, e.g. the quality of parts received by an activity is a determining factor in the work required by that activity and therefore affects the resources required. An activity may have multiple cost drivers associated with it (CAM–I).

cost estimation

The determination of cost behaviour. This can be achieved by engineering methods, analysis of the accounts, by use of statistics or by the pooling of expert views.

cost management

The application of management accounting concepts, methods of data collection, analysis and presentation, in order to provide the information required to enable costs to be planned, monitored and controlled.

cost object

See cost unit.

cost pool

The point of focus for the costs relating to a particular activity in an activity-based costing system

cost of quality

The difference between the actual cost of producing, selling and sup-

FIGURE 3.6 BUDGETED TRADING AND PROFIT AND LOSS ACCOUNTS, ABSORPTION COSTING AND MARGINAL COSTING

ABSORPTION COSTING		MARGINAL COSTING		
	Net turnover		Net turnover	
less:		less:		
Direct Materials		Direct Materials		
Direct Labour		Direct Labour		
Total Production Overhead	Production Cost of Sales	Variable Production Overhead		
		Variable Selling and Distribution Overhead	Variable Cost of Sales	
	Gross (or Factory) Profit			
			Contribution	
Less:		Less *fixed costs:*		
Selling Overhead		Production Overhead		
Distribution Overhead		Selling Overhead		
Administrative Expenses		Distribution Overhead		
		Administrative Expenses		
R&D Cost	Non-production Overhead	R&D Cost	Total Fixed Cost	
	Net Profit before Tax		Net Profit before Tax	

* Note: In an "actual" absorption costing based Trading and Profit and Loss Account, production overhead would normally be over- or under-absorbed, due to both cost and activity levels differing from those upon which the budget was based.

An over-absorption occurs when overhead costs absorbed by output exceed the actual costs incurred.

An under-absorption occurs when the actual costs incurred exceed the overhead costs absorbed by output.

FIGURE 3.7 COST BEHAVIOUR

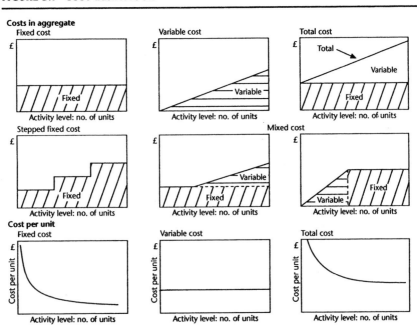

FIGURE 3.8 ASSESSMENT OF FIXED COST ELEMENT BY THE USE OF A SCATTERGRAPH

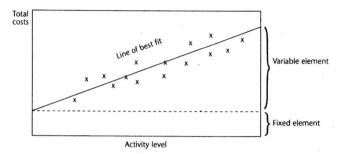

The use of a scattergraph gives no indication of the direction of the cause and effect relationship, nor does it accurately measure the strength of the relationship. Further, by being interpreted visually, its use is subject to considerable risk of error.

porting products or services and the equivalent costs if there were no failures during production or usage. The cost of quality can be analysed into:

cost of conformance
The cost of achieving specified quality standards.

- ◆ *cost of prevention* – the costs incurred prior to or during production in order to prevent substandard or defective products or services from being produced.
- ◆ *cost of appraisal* – costs incurred in order to ensure that outputs produced meet required quality standards.

cost of non-conformance
The cost of failure to deliver the required standard of quality.

- ◆ *cost of internal failure* – the costs arising from inadequate quality which are identified before the transfer of ownership from supplier to purchaser.
- ◆ *cost of external failure* – the cost arising from inadequate quality discovered after the transfer of ownership from supplier to purchaser.

Note: There is no universally accepted definition of quality, which may be assessed on a number of bases, such as (a) conformance to specification, (b) ability to satisfy wants, (c) inclusion of attractive performance/aesthetic attributes or (d) offering value for money.

cost reduction
The reduction in unit cost of goods or services without impairing suitability for the use intended.

cost table
A database containing all the costs associated with the production of a product, broken down to include the costs of functions and/or components and sub-assemblies. Cost tables also incorporate the cost changes which would result from a number of possible changes in the input mix.

cost unit
A unit of product or service in relation to which costs are ascertained. *See* Figure 3.9.

costing
The process of determining the costs of products, services or activities.

absorption costing
A method of costing that, in addition to direct costs, assigns all, or a proportion of, production overhead

FIGURE 3.9 COST UNITS

Examples of cost units

Industry sector	Cost unit
Brewing	Barrel
Brick-making	1,000 bricks
Coal mining	Tonne/ton
Electricity	Kilowatt hour (KwH)
Engineering	Contract, job
Oil	Barrel, tonne, litre
Hotel/catering	Room/cover
Professional services	Chargeable hour, job, contract
Education	Course, enrolled student, successful student
Hospitals	Patient episode

Activity	Cost unit
Credit control	Account maintained
Materials storage/handling	Requisition unit issued/received, material movement value issued/received
Personnel administration	Personnel record
Selling	Customer call, value of sales, orders taken

FIGURE 3.10 ELEMENTS OF AN ABSORPTION COSTING SYSTEM

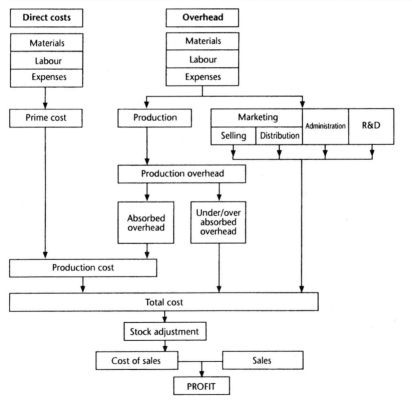

Notes: 1. The above chart is based on the absorption costing principle.
2. In the case of marginal costing, the amount of production overhead absorbed would relate to the variable element only.
3. The relative sizes of the boxes are of no significance

costs to cost units by means of one or a number of *overhead absorption rates. See* Figure 3.4.

batch costing
A form of specific order costing in which costs are attributed to batches of products. *See* Figure 3.1.

continuous operation/process costing
The costing method applicable where goods or services result from a sequence of continuous or repetitive operations or processes. Costs are averaged over the units produced during the period, being initially charged to the operation or process. *See* Figure 3.1.

contract costing
A form of specific order costing in which costs are attributed to individual contracts. *See* Figure 3.1.

job costing
A form of specific order costing in which costs are attributed to individual jobs. *See* Figure 3.1.

marginal costing
The accounting system in which variable costs are charged to cost units and fixed costs of the period are written off in full against the aggregate contribution. Its special value is in recognising cost behaviour, and hence assisting in decision-making. *See* Figure 3.6.

service/function costing
Cost accounting for services or functions, e.g. canteens, maintenance, personnel. These may be referred to as service centres, departments or functions. *See* Figure 3.1.

specific order costing
The basic cost accounting method applicable where work consists of separately identifiable contracts, jobs or batches. *See* Figure 3.1.

standard costing
A control technique which compares standard costs and revenues with actual results to obtain variances which are used to stimulate improved performance.

uniform costing
The use by several undertakings of the same costing systems, i.e. the same basic costing methods, principles and techniques.

critical success factor
An element of organisational activity which is central to its future success. Critical success factors may change over time, and may include items such as product quality, employee attitudes, manufacturing flexibility, and brand awareness.

customer profitability analysis (CPA)
Analysis of the revenue streams and service costs associated with specific customers or customer groups.

cycle time
The total time taken from the start of the production of a product or service to its completion. Cycle time includes processing time, move time, wait time and inspection time, only the first of which creates value.

differential/incremental cost
The difference in total cost between alternatives; calculated to assist decision-making.

direct cost
Expenditure which can be economically identified with and specifically measured in respect to a relevant cost object. *See* Figure 3.4.

direct product profitability (DPP)
Used primarily within the retail sector, DPP involves the attribution of costs other than the purchase price (e.g. distribution, warehousing, retailing) to each product line. Thus a net profit, as opposed to a

gross profit, can be identified for each product. The cost attribution process utilises a variety of measures (e.g. warehousing space, transport time) to reflect the resource consumption of individual products.

discretionary cost

A cost whose amount within a time period is determined by, and is easily altered by, a decision taken by the appropriate budget holder. Marketing, research and training are generally regarded as discretionary costs. Control of discretionary costs is through the budgeting process. Also known as *managed* or *policy* costs.

diverted hours

The available hours of nominally direct workers who are diverted to indirect activities, e.g. cleaning machines, and are therefore charged as indirect labour. This contrasts with indirect workers whose entire time is charged as indirect.

The alternative expressions *directs on indirect work, indirect hours* or *diversions* are not recommended.

downsizing

Organisational restructuring involving outsourcing activities, replacing permanent staff with contract employees and reducing the number of levels within the organisational hierarchy, with the intention of making the organisation more flexible, efficient and responsive to its environment.

economic order quantity (EOQ)

The most economic stock replenishment order size, which minimises the sum of stock ordering costs and stockholding costs. EOQ is used in an 'optimising' stock control system.

EOQ may be calculated as:

$$\sqrt{\frac{2C_0 D}{C_h}}$$

Where
D   is demand for a time period
C_0 is the cost of placing one order
C_h is the cost of holding one item for that time period

elements of cost

The constituent parts of costs according to the factors upon which expenditure is incurred, namely, material, labour and expenses. See Figure 3.10.

engineered cost

A cost which varies in proportion to a measure of activity. Direct materials and royalty payments are engineered costs. Control is through flexible budgeting or standard costing.

equivalent units

Notional whole units representing uncompleted work. Used to apportion costs between work in progress and completed output, and in performance assessment.

facility-sustaining activities

Activities undertaken to support the organisation as a whole, and which cannot be logically linked to individual units of output. Accounting is a facility-sustaining activity. See hierarchy of activities.

feasible region

The area contained within all of the constraint lines shown on a graphical depiction of a linear programming problem. All feasible combinations of output are contained within or located on the boundaries of the feasible region. See Figure 3.11.

first in, first out (FIFO)

The principle that the oldest items or costs are the first to be used. Most commonly applied to the pricing of issues of materials, based on using first the costs of the oldest materials in stock, *irrespective of the sequence in which actual material usage takes place.* Closing stock is therefore generally valued at relatively current costs. *See* Figure 3.12.

FIGURE 3.11: FEASIBLE REGION

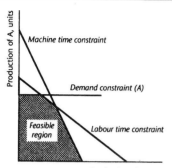

fixed cost

A cost which is incurred for an accounting period, and which, within certain output or turnover limits, tends to be unaffected by fluctuations in the levels of activity (output or turnover).

flexible manufacturing system (FMS)

An integrated, computer-controlled production system which is capable of producing any of a range of parts, and of switching quickly and economically between them.

free stock

Stock on hand or on order which has not been scheduled for use. (physical stock + stock ordered – stock scheduled)

functional analysis

An analysis of the relationships between product functions, their perceived value to the customer and their cost of provision.

hierarchy of activities

Classification of activities according to the level within the organisation to which they relate. A common classification is as product level activities, batch level activities, product sustaining activities, and facility sustaining activities.

high/low method

Method of estimating cost behaviour by comparing the total costs associated with two different levels of

FIGURE 3.12 PRICING OF STOCK ISSUES

Date	Purchase quantity	Unit cost	Total cost	Issue quantity	Issue cost	Balance	
	Units	£	£	Units	£	Units	£
1 April	200	1.20	240	—	—	200	240
12 April	350	1.30	455	—	—	550	695
13 April	420	1.10	462	—	—	970	1,157
15 April	—			500	(a)	470	(b)

The valuation of the issues made on 15 April (a) and the valuation of the residual stock (b) are as follows

Valuation of issues: *Valuation of residual stock:*

FIFO: (200 × £1.20) + (300 × £1.30) = £630   £527

LIFO: (420 × £1.10) + (80 × £1.30) = £566   £591

Weighted average: $(500 \times {}^{£1,157}/_{970}) = £596$ £561

Note: The valuation of stock issues is independent of any policy with respect to the order in which physical stock should be issued, which would, where practicable, be FIFO.

output. The difference in costs is assumed to be caused by variable costs increasing, allowing unit variable cost to be calculated. Following from this, since total cost is known, the fixed cost can be derived.

holding cost
The cost of retaining an asset, generally stock. Holding cost includes the cost of financing the asset in addition to the cost of physical storage.

incremental analysis
Analysis of the changes in costs and revenues caused by a change in activity. Normally the technique is used where a significant volume change occurs, causing changes to both variable and fixed costs and possibly to selling prices. Incremental or differential costs and revenues are compared to determine the financial effect of the activity change.

ISO 9000
A quality system standard which requires complying organisations to operate in accordance with a structure of written policies and procedures that are designed to ensure the consistent delivery of a product or service to meet customer requirements.

job
A customer order or task of relatively short duration.

job cost sheet
A detailed record of the amount, and cost, of the labour, material and overhead charged to a specific job.

joint cost
The cost of a process which results in more than one main product.

joint products
Two or more products produced by the same process and separated in processing, each having a sufficiently high saleable value to merit

recognition as a main product. See by-product.

just-in-time (JIT)
A system whose objective is to produce or to procure products or components as they are required by a customer or for use, rather than for stock. A just-in-time system is a 'pull' system, which responds to demand, in contrast to a 'push' system, in which stocks act as buffers between the different elements of the system, such as purchasing, production and sales.

just-in-time production
A production system which is driven by demand for finished products whereby each component on a production line is produced only when needed for the next stage.

just-in-time purchasing
A purchasing system in which material purchases are contracted so that the receipt and usage of material, to the maximum extent possible, coincide.

kaizen
A Japanese term for continuous improvement in all aspects of a company's performance, at every level.

last in, first out (LIFO)
A little-used method of pricing the issue of material using the purchase price of the latest unit in stock. More often, in the USA, a method of valuing stock using indices to charge most recent prices against profits. *See* Figure 3.12.

lead time
The time interval between the start of an activity or process and its completion, e.g. the time between ordering goods and their receipt, or between starting production of a product and its completion. The latter is also known as *process time*.

FIGURE 3.13 LEARNING CURVE

Example:

A team of technicians has assembled the first of a new model of aircraft engine in a total of 2,000 hours. Assuming an 80% learning curve, determine:

1. How long it will take to manufacture the next engine
2. How long it will take to manufacture the next three engines
3. Having already produced two engines, the average time per engine required for the next six

Engines	Cumulative Engines	Average hours	Cumulative hours per engine
1	1	2,000	2,000
1	2	1,600 (2,000 × 0.8)	3,200
2	4	1,280 (1,600 × 0.8)	5,120
4	8	1,024 (1,280 × 0.8)	8,192

1. The next engine will take (3,200 − 2,000) hours = 1,200 hours
2. The next three engines will take (5,120 − 2,000) hours = 3,120 hours
3. (8,192 − 3,200)/6 = 832 hours

Average time per unit

The Learning Curve

Output

The learning curve can also be expressed mathematically as:

$$Y = \frac{a}{x^\beta}$$

Where Y is the average time taken per unit/batch to produce a cumulative number of units/batches:

a is the time required to produce the first unit
x is the cumulative number of units to be produced
β is the coefficient of learning, which can be calculated as:

$$- \frac{\text{logarithm of rate of learning*}}{\text{logarithm of 2.0}}$$

* for an 80% learning curve, this would be log 0.8

learning curve

The mathematical expression of the phenomenon that when complex and labour-intensive procedures are repeated, unit labour times tend to decrease at a constant rate. The learning curve models mathematically this reduction in unit production time. The learning curve is also known as the *experience curve*. *See* Figure 3.13.

life cycle costing

The maintenance of physical asset cost records over the entire asset lives, so that decisions concerning the acquisition, use or disposal of the assets can be made in a way that achieves the optimum asset usage at the lowest possible cost to the entity. The term may be applied to the profiling of cost over a product's life, including the pre-production stage (*terotechnology*), and to both company and industry life cycles. *See* Figure 3.14.

lost time record

A record of the time a machine or employee is not producing, usually stating reasons and responsibilities. Lost time can include waiting time and maintenance.

manufacturing resource planning (MRP II)

An expansion of material requirements planning (MRP I) to give a broader approach than MRP I to the planning and scheduling of resources, embracing areas such as finance, logistics, engineering and marketing.

FIGURE 3.14 LIFE CYCLE COSTS OF A PRODUCT OR SERVICE

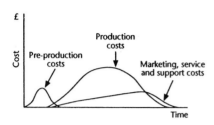

marginal cost
The part of the cost of one unit of product or service which would be avoided if that unit were not produced, or which would increase if one extra unit were produced.

marginal revenue
The additional revenue generated from the sale of one additional unit of output.

mark-up
The difference between the selling price and cost of sales, expressed either as a percentage of the cost of sales or as an absolute amount.

material requirements planning (MRP I)
A system that converts a production schedule into a listing of the materials and components required to meet that schedule, so that adequate stock levels are maintained and items are available when needed.

materials/stores requisition
A document which authorises the issue from store of a specified quantity of materials.

materials transfer note
A record of the transfer of material between stores, cost centres, or cost units.

maximum stock level
A stock level, set for control purposes, which actual stockholding should never exceed. ((reorder level + EOQ) – (minimum rate of usage × minimum lead time))

minimum stock level
A stock level, set for control purposes, below which stockholding should not fall without being highlighted. (reorder level – (average rate of usage × average lead time))

move time
The time taken in moving a product between locations during the production process. *See* cycle time.

normal loss
An expected loss, allowed for in the budget, and normally calculated as a percentage of the good output from a process during a period of time. Normal losses are generally either valued at zero, or at their disposal values.

notional cost
A cost used in product evaluation, decision-making and performance measurement to represent the cost of using resources which have no conventional 'actual cost'. Notional interest, for example, may be charged for the use of internally generated funds.

operational gearing
The relationship of the fixed cost to the total cost of an operating unit. The greater the proportion of total costs that are fixed (high operational gearing), the greater is the advantage to the organisation of increasing sales volume. Conversely, should sales volumes drop, a highly geared organisation would find the high proportion of fixed costs to be a major problem, possibly causing a rapid swing from profitability into significant loss-making. Gearing may also be referred to as leverage. *See* gearing/leverage (Chapter 7).

opportunity cost

The value of the benefit sacrificed when one course of action is chosen, in preference to an alternative. The opportunity cost is represented by the forgone potential benefit from the best rejected course of action.

outsourcing

The use of external suppliers as a source of finished products, components or services. This is also known as contract manufacturing or subcontracting.

overhead/indirect cost

Expenditure on labour, materials or services which cannot be economically identified with a specific saleable cost unit. *See* Figure 3.9.

The synonymous term 'burden' is in common use in the USA and in subsidiaries of American companies in the UK.

overhead absorption rate

A means of attributing overhead to a product or service, based for example on direct labour hours, direct labour cost or machine hours.

direct labour cost percentage rate
An overhead absorption rate based on direct labour cost.

direct labour hour rate
An overhead absorption rate based on direct labour hours.

machine hour rate
An overhead absorption rate based on machine hours. The choice of overhead absorption base may be made with the objective of obtaining 'accurate' product costs, or of influencing managerial behaviour, as where overhead applied to (say) labour hours or part numbers appears to make the use of these resources more costly, thus discouraging their use.
See Figure 3.4.

payroll

A record showing for each employee, gross pay, deductions and net pay.

It may also include details of the employer's associated employment costs.

payroll analysis

An analysis of a payroll for cost accounting purposes, giving, e.g.
♦ gross pay by department or operation;
♦ gross pay by class of labour;
♦ gross pay by product;
♦ constituent parts of gross pay, e.g. direct pay and lost time.

period cost

A cost which relates to a time period rather than to the output of products or services.

perpetual inventory

The recording as they occur of receipts, issues, and the resulting balances of individual items of stock in either quantity or quantity and value.

physical stocktaking

The actual ascertainment of stocks held (by physical counting) for comparison with accounting records. Modern practice is to stocktake different items with different frequencies, classifying items according to the degree of control required. *Periodic stocktaking* is a process whereby all stock items are physically counted and valued at a set point in time, usually the end of an accounting period.
Continuous stocktaking is the process of counting and valuing selected items at different times, on a rotating basis.

post-purchase costs

Costs incurred after a capital expenditure decision has been implemented and facilities acquired. These costs may include training, maintenance and the cost of upgrades.

prime cost

The total cost of direct material, direct labour and direct expenses.

product cost

The cost of a finished product built up from its cost elements.

product-sustaining activities

Activities undertaken in support of production, the costs of which are linked to the number of separate products produced rather than to the volume of output. Engineering change is a product-sustaining activity. *See* hierarchy of activities.

production cost

Prime cost plus absorbed production overhead.

project costing

See costing, contract costing.

quality assurance

Ensuring products or services consistently meet quality specifications.

reciprocal cost allocation

Method of secondary cost allocation generally used to reallocate service department costs over the user departments. Service department costs are recharged over user departments (including other service depts) in a number of iterations until all of the service dept costs have been re-charged to users.

recovery

See overhead absorption rate.

rejects/defects

Units of output which fail a set quality standard and are subsequently rectified, sold as substandard or disposed of as scrap.

relevant costs/revenues

Costs and revenues appropriate to a specific management decision. These are represented by future cash flows whose magnitude will vary depending upon the outcome of the management decision made. If stock is sold by a retailer, the relevant cost, used in the determination of the profitability of the transaction, would be the cost of replacing the stock, not its original purchase price, which is a sunk cost. *Abandonment analysis*, based on relevant cost and revenues, is the process of determining whether or not it is more profitable to discontinue a product or service than to continue it.

reorder level

A level of stock at which a replenishment order should be placed. Traditional 'optimising' systems use a variation on the following computation, which builds in a measure of safety stock and minimises the likelihood of a stock out. (maximum usage × maximum lead)

replacement price

The price at which identical goods or capital equipment could be purchased at the date of valuation.

resource drivers

Measurement units which are used to assign resource costs to activity cost pools based on some measure of usage. Thus area may be used to assign office occupancy costs to purchasing, accounting services etc.

reverse engineering

The decomposition and analysis of competitors' products in order to determine how they are made, costs of production and the way in which future development may proceed.

safety stock

Quantity of stocks of raw materials, work in progress and finished goods which are carried in excess of the expected usage during the lead time of an activity. The safety stock reduces the probability of operations having to be suspended due to running out of stocks.

scrap

Discarded material having some value.

semi-variable cost/semi-fixed cost/mixed cost

A cost containing both fixed and variable components and which is thus partly affected by a change in the level of activity.

shared services

A business strategy which involves centralising certain business activities such as accounting and other transaction-oriented activities in order to reduce costs and provide better customer service.

simultaneous/concurrent engineering

A means of reducing product development time and cost by managing development processes so that they can be implemented simultaneously (rather than sequentially).

strategic business unit

A section, within a larger organisation, responsible for planning, developing, producing and marketing its own products or services.

sunk costs

Costs that have been irreversibly incurred or committed prior to a decision point and which cannot therefore be considered relevant to subsequent decisions. Sunk costs may also be termed *irrecoverable costs*.

target cost

A product cost estimate derived by subtracting a desired profit margin from a competitive market price. This may be less than the planned initial product cost, but will be expected to be achieved by the time the product reaches the mature production stage.

theory of constraints (TOC)

An approach to production management which aims to maximise sales revenue less material and variable overhead cost. It focuses on factors such as bottlenecks which act as constraints to this maximisation.

throughput

(i) The rate of production of a defined process over a stated period of time. Rates may be expressed in terms of units of products, batches produced, turnover, or other meaningful measurements (CAM–I).

(ii) A performance measurement used to determine performance achievement towards the goal of the organisation and to judge the impact of a local action or a local decision on the overall performance of the system as a whole. For profit-focused organisations, it means the rate at which money is generated (usually through sales). When trading through sales, this is the net amount generated by the organisation and is the difference between the money obtained from customers (selling price) minus all the money paid to the vendors and suppliers (raw materials, bought-in parts, direct services and direct commissions). Specifically throughput does not consider any expenses associated with labour, direct or indirect (Goldratt Institute).

throughput accounting

A management accounting system which focuses on ways by which the maximum return per unit of bottleneck activity can be achieved.

time

breaking-down time

The period required to return a workstation to a standard condition after completion of an operation (BS 5191).

changeover time
The period required to change a workstation from a state of readiness for one operation to a state of readiness for another (BS 5191).

cycle time
The period required to complete an operation on one unit of a batch (BS 5191).

downtime
The period for which a workstation is not available for production due to a functional failure (BS 5191).

idle time
The period for which a workstation is available for production but is not used due to, e.g., shortage of tooling, material or operators (BS 5191).

lead time
The time expected to elapse between the start of a process or activity and its completion.

operation time
The period required to carry out an operation on a complete batch exclusive of set-up and breaking-down times (BS 5191).

process time
The period which elapses between the start and finish of one process or stage of a process.

queuing time
The time between the arrival of material at a workstation and the start of work on it (BS 5191).

set-up time
The period required to prepare a workstation from a standard condition to readiness to commence a specified operation (BS 5191).

standard time
The total time in which a task should be completed by employees working at standard levels of efficiency.

transit time
The period between the completion of an operation and the availability of the material at the succeeding workstation (BS 5191).

waiting time
The period for which an operator is available for production but is prevented from working by shortage of material or tooling or machine breakdown (BS 5191).

time sheet
A record of how a person's time has been spent. Used to calculate pay, to assess the efficient use of time or to charge for work done.

total quality management (TQM)
An integrated and comprehensive system of planning and controlling all business functions so that products or services are produced which meet or exceed customer expectations. TQM is a philosophy of business behaviour, embracing principles such as employee involvement, continuous improvement at all levels and customer focus, as well as being a collection of related techniques aimed at improving quality such as full documentation of activities, clear goal-setting and performance measurement from the customer perspective.

transfer price
The price at which goods or services are transferred between different units of the same company. If those units are located within different countries, the term *international transfer pricing* is used.

The extent to which the transfer price covers costs and contributes to (internal) profit is a matter of policy. A transfer price may, for example, be based upon marginal cost, full cost, market price or negotiation. Where the transferred products cross national boundaries, the transfer prices used may have to be agreed with the governments of the countries concerned.

value analysis

A systematic interdisciplinary examination of factors affecting the cost of a product or service, in order to devise means of achieving the specified purpose most economically at the required standard of quality and reliability (BS 3138).

value chain

The sequence of business activities by which, in the perspective of the end user, value is added to the products or services produced by an organisation.

value driver

An activity or organisational focus which enhances the perceived value of a product or service in the perception of the consumer, and which therefore creates value for the producer. Advanced technology, reliability or reputation for customer care may be value drivers.

value engineering

An activity which helps to design products which meet customer needs at the lowest cost while assuring the required standard of quality and reliability.

variable cost

A cost which varies with a measure of activity.

waste

Discarded material having no value.

weighted average cost

A method of unit cost determination, often applied to stocks, in which an average unit cost is calculated, when a new purchase quantity is received, by dividing the sum of the cost of the opening stock plus the cost of the acquisitions, by the total number of units in stock. *See* Figure 3.12

work cell

A group of employees or of machines dedicated to performing a specific manufacturing task, or group of related tasks.

world class manufacturing

A position of international manufacturing excellence, achieved by developing a culture based on factors such as continuous improvement, problem prevention, zero defect tolerance, customer-driven JIT-based production and total quality management.

CHAPTER 4

◆

Planning

Boston Consulting Group matrix

A representation of an organisation's product or service offerings which shows the value of each product sales (depicted by the area of a circle) expressed in relation to the growth rate of the market served and the market share held. The objective of the matrix is to assist in the allocation of funds to projects. *See* Figure 4.1.

FIGURE 4.1 BOSTON CONSULTING GROUP MATRIX

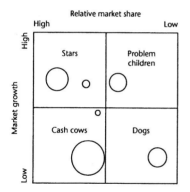

breakeven chart

A chart which indicates approximate profit or loss at different levels of sales volume within a limited range.

For examples of conventional breakeven charts under different cost structures, *see* Figures 4.2 and 4.3. Figure 4.4 shows a contribution breakeven chart and Figure 4.5 a profit–volume chart.

breakeven point

The level of activity at which there

is neither profit nor loss. It can be ascertained by using a breakeven chart or by calculation.

Example:

	£
Sales	10,000
Variable costs	
(e.g. direct materials, direct labour)	6,000
Contribution	4,000
Fixed cost	2,000
Profit	2,000

Number of units sold   1,000
Contribution per unit   £4

Contribution to sales ratio

$$\frac{£4,000}{£10,000} \times 100 = 40\%$$

Number of units to be sold to break even

$$\frac{\text{Total fixed cost}}{\text{Contribution per unit}} = \frac{£2,000}{£4} = 500 \text{ units}$$

Sales value at breakeven point

$$\frac{\text{Total fixed cost}}{\text{Contribution to sales ratio}} = \frac{£2,000}{40\%} = £5,000$$

Time to break even

$$\frac{\text{Total fixed cost} \times 365 =}{\text{Total contribution}} \frac{£2,000}{£4,000} \times 365 = 6 \text{ mth}$$

(assuming that the period is one year, and that the rate of sales is constant within that period)

cash cow

A product characterised by a high market share but low sales growth, whose function is seen as generating cash for use elsewhere within the organisation.

competitive position

The market share, costs, prices, quality and accumulated experience of an entity or product relative to competition.

FIGURE 4.2 CONVENTIONAL BREAKEVEN CHART I

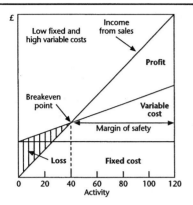

FIGURE 4.3 CONVENTIONAL BREAKEVEN CHART II

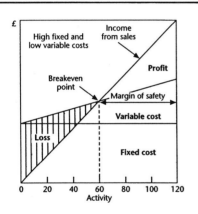

FIGURE 4.4 CONTRIBUTION BREAKEVEN CHART

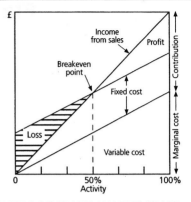

FIGURE 4.5 PROFIT–VOLUME CHART

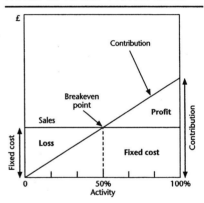

FIGURE 4.6 THE COMPETITIVE SAW

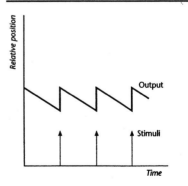

competitive saw

Illustration of the principle that every investment in a product, while initially improving the reported performance in relation to competitors, eventually degrades and has to be succeeded by further investment(s) to maintain the competitive position. *See* Figure 4.6.

contingency plan

Action to be implemented only upon the occurrence of anticipated future events other than those in the accepted plan.

FIGURE 4.7 DECISION TREE

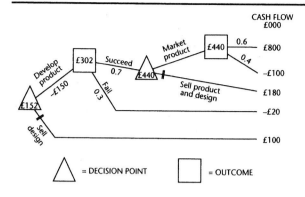

CASH FLOW
£000

The decision tree shows the cash flows associated with the activities of (i) developing a product and (ii) selling the design. Problems are solved using decision trees by working from right to left. The decision tree on the left shows that the optimum course of action is to develop the product, generating a cash flow of £152,000, which is better than the alternative of selling the design, which generates £100,000.

△ = DECISION POINT   □ = OUTCOME

corporate appraisal

A critical assessment of the strengths and weaknesses, opportunities and threats (SWOT analysis) in relation to the internal and environmental factors affecting an entity in order to establish its condition prior to the preparation of the long-term plan.

cost-volume-profit analysis (CVP)

The study of the effects on future profit of changes in fixed cost, variable cost, sales price, quantity and mix.

decision tree

A pictorial method of showing a sequence of interrelated decisions and their expected outcomes. Decision trees can incorporate both the probabilities of, and values of, expected outcomes, and are used in decision-making. See Figure 4.7.

forecast

A prediction of future events and their quantification for planning purposes.

gap analysis

A comparison between an entity's ultimate objective (most commonly expressed in terms of demand, but may be reported in terms of profit, ROCE etc.) and the expected performance of projects both planned and under way. Differences are classified in a way which aids the understanding of performance, and

FIGURE 4.8 GAP ANALYSIS – EXISTING PRODUCTS

Demand gap: the difference between total market potential and current demand from users.
Distribution gap: loss of product demand due to lack of access to or utilisation of distribution channels.
Product gap: the proportion of market demand lost through product failure or deliberate product-positioning decisions.
Competitive gap: loss in sales due to factors such as failures in pricing or promotion.

which facilitates improvement. *See* Figure 4.8.

goal congruence

In a control system, the state which leads individuals or groups to take actions which are in their self-interest and also in the best interest of the entity.

Goal incongruence exists when the interests of individuals or of groups associated with an entity are not in harmony.

limiting factor or key factor

Anything which limits the activity of an entity. An entity seeks to optimise the benefit it obtains from the limiting factor.

Examples are a shortage of supply of a resource or a restriction on sales demand at a particular price.

market share

One entity's sales of a product or service in a specified market expressed as a proportion of total sales by all entities offering that product or service to the market. A planning tool and a performance assessment ratio.

maximax criterion

An approach to decision-making under uncertainty in which an 'optimistic' view of the possible outcome is adopted. The favoured strategy is therefore to implement the course of action which leads to the highest possible profit, irrespective of (a) the probability of that profit actually being achieved, and (b) the outcome if it is not successful. A risk-taker may make decisions on this basis.

maximin criterion

An approach to decision-making under uncertainty in which a 'pessimistic' view of the possible outcome is adopted. The favoured strategy is therefore to implement

the course of action whose worst possible outcome generates the highest profit. This basis for decision-making characterises risk-averse decision-makers.

minimax regret criterion

An approach to decision-making under uncertainty in which the opportunity cost (regret) associated with each possible course of action is measured, and the decision-maker selects the activity which minimises the maximum regret, or loss. Regret is measured as the difference between the best and worst possible payoff for each option.

network analysis

A quantitative technique used in project control. The events and activities making up the whole project are represented in the form of a diagram. *See* Figure 4.9.

critical event

Any event which lies on the critical path. *See* Figure 4.9.

critical path

The longest path or paths through a network. *See* Figure 4.9.

event

The start or completion of an activity. In a network an event is represented by a small circle (a node), and an activity by an arrow.

project evaluation and review technique (PERT)

A specification of all activities, events, probabilities and constraints relating to a project, from which a network is drawn, providing a model of the way the project should proceed.

slack/float time

The time available for an activity over and above that required for its completion.

operations plans

The fully detailed specifications by

FIGURE 4.9 CRITICAL PATH IN A SIMPLE NETWORK

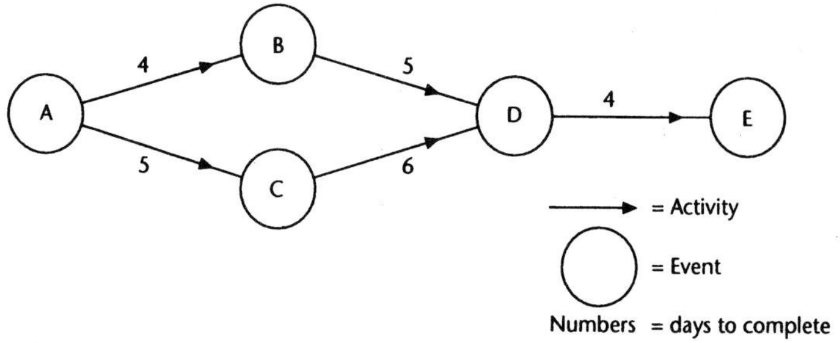

The critical path is A to C to D to E = 15 days
The slack for A to B to D = A to C to D – A to B to D = 2 days

which individuals are expected to carry out the predetermined cycles of operations to meet sectoral objectives.

Pareto (80/20) distribution

A frequency distribution with a small proportion (say 20 per cent) of the items accounting for a large proportion (say 80 per cent) of the value/resources. Common occurrences are:

- sales, when 80 per cent of turnover may arise from 20 per cent of customers;
- stock, when 80 per cent of the value may comprise 20 per cent of the items. *See* Figure 4.10.

FIGURE 4.10 PARETO (80/20) DISTRIBUTION: STOCK

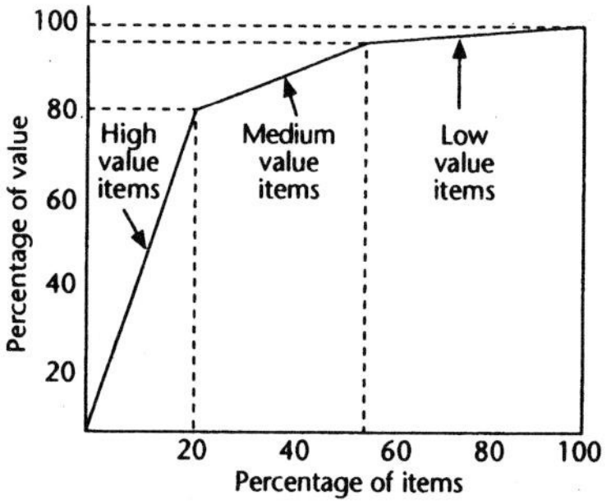

planning

The establishment of objectives, and the formulation, evaluation and selection of the policies, strategies, tactics and action required to achieve them. Planning comprises long-term/strategic planning, and short-term operation planning. The latter is usually for a period of up to one year.

capital funding planning

The process of selecting suitable funds to finance long-term assets and working capital.

capital resource planning

The process of evaluating and selecting long-term assets to meet strategies.

financial planning

Planning the acquisition of funds to finance planned activities.

futuristic planning

Planning for that period which extends beyond the planning horizon in the form of future expected conditions which may exist in respect of the entity, products/services and environment but which cannot usefully be expressed in quantified terms. An example would be working out the actions needed in a future with no motor cars.

strategic planning

The formulation, evaluation and selection of strategies for the purpose of preparing a long-term plan of action to attain objectives. Also known as *corporate planning* and *long-range planning*.

tactical planning

Planning the utilisation of resources to achieve specific objectives in the most effective and efficient way.

planning horizon

The furthest time ahead for which plans can be quantified. It need not be the planning period. *See* planning, futuristic planning.

planning period

The period for which a plan is prepared and used. It differs according to product or process life cycle. For example, forestry requires a period of many years whereas fashion garments require only a few months.

policy

An undated, long-lasting and often unquantified statement of guidance regarding the way in which an organisation will seek to behave in relation to its stakeholders.

position audit

Part of the planning process which examines the current state of the entity in respect of:
- resources of tangible and intangible assets and finance;
- products, brands and markets;
- operating systems such as production and distribution;
- internal organisation;
- current results;
- returns to stockholders.

product life cycle

The period which begins with the initial product specification, and ends with the withdrawal from the market of both the product and its support. It is characterised by defined stages including research, development, introduction, maturity, decline and abandonment (Cam–I adapted). *See* Figure 3.14.

profit–volume/contribution graph

Graph showing the effect on contribution and on overall profit of changes in sales volume or value. *See* Figure 4.5.

programming

dynamic programming

An operational research technique used to solve multi-stage problems in which the decisions at one stage are the accepted assumptions applicable to the next stage.

linear programming

The use of a series of linear equations to construct a mathematical model. The objective is to obtain an optimal solution to a complex operational problem, which may involve the production of a number of products in an environment in which there are many constraints.

non-linear programming

A process in which the equations expressing the interactions of variables are not all linear but may, for example, be in proportion to the square of a variable.

projection

An expected future trend pattern obtained by extrapolation. It is principally concerned with quantitative factors, whereas a forecast includes judgements. *See* Figure 4.11.

rolling forecast

A continuously updated forecast whereby each time actual results are reported, a further forecast period is added and intermediate period forecasts are updated. *See* rolling budget (Chapter 5).

sensitivity analysis

A modelling and risk assessment

FIGURE 4.11 PROJECTION

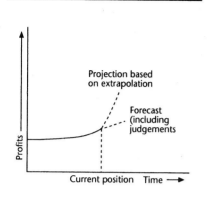

procedure in which changes are made to significant variables in order to determine the effect of these changes on the planned outcome. Particular attention is thereafter paid to variables identified as being of special significance.

shadow price

An increase in value which would be created by having available one additional unit of a limiting resource at its original cost. This represents the opportunity cost of not having the use of the one extra unit. This information is routinely produced when mathematical programming (especially linear programming) is used to model activity.

FIGURE 4.12 POLICIES, STRATEGIES, TACTICS AND OPERATIONAL CONTROL

Example	Industry	Services
Policies	To produce products which are technically superior to the competition	To offer a service at a cost to the consumer which is consistently lower than offered by competitors. To reinforce the brand name of the company at every opportunity
Strategy	To spend 15% + of gross revenue on R & D	Consistently utilise the most innovative marketing devices, at all levels Set service prices locally, such that the competition is always beaten on price
Tactics	Recruit from the best university technology courses Gain BS EN ISO 9000 accreditation. Set up cross departmental working groups.	Use cost reducing technology wherever possible Implement brand awareness surveys Reinforce volume by offering 'special deals'.
Operational control	Monitor feedback on all programmes attended. Integrate training needs programmes attended	Develop customer questionnaires to aid assessment of quality. Use budget/actual cash flow comparisons to achieve control of operating units

slack variables

The amount of each resource which will be unused if a specific linear programming solution is implemented.

strategic management accounting

A form of management accounting in which emphasis is placed on information which relates to factors external to the firm, as well as non-financial information and internally generated information.

strategic plan

A statement of long-term goals along with a definition of the strategies and policies which will ensure achievement of these goals.

strategy

A course of action, including the specification of resources required, to achieve a specific objective. *See* Figure 4.12.

tactical plan/tactics

Short-term plan for achieving an entity's objectives. *See* Figure 4.12.

CHAPTER 5

❖

Budgeting

activity-based budgeting

A method of budgeting based on an activity framework and utilising cost driver data in the budget-setting and variance feedback processes.

budget

A quantitative statement, for a defined period of time, which may include planned revenues, expenses, assets, liabilities and cash flows. A budget provides a focus for the organisation, aids the co-ordination of activities, and facilitates control. Planning is achieved by means of a fixed *master budget*, whereas control is generally exercised through the comparison of actual costs with a *flexible budget*. *See* zero-based budgeting, rolling/continuous budget, participative budgeting, negotiated budget.

budget centre

A section of an entity for which control may be exercised and budgets prepared.

budget cost allowance/flexed budget

The budgeted cost ascribed to the level of activity achieved in a budget centre in a control period. It comprises variable costs in direct proportion to volume achieved and fixed costs as a proportion of the annual budget.

budget lapsing

Withdrawal of unspent budget allowance due to the expiry of the budget period.

budget manual

A detailed set of documents providing guidelines and information

about the budget process. A budget manual may include:

◆ a calendar of budgetary events;
◆ specimen budget forms;
◆ a statement of budgetary objective and desired results;
◆ a listing of budgetary activities;
◆ original, revised and approved budgets;
◆ budget assumptions regarding inflation, interest rates etc.

budget period

The period for which a budget is prepared and used, which may then be subdivided into control periods.

budget slack

The intentional overestimation of expenses and/or underestimation of revenues in the budgeting process.

budgetary control

The establishment of budgets relating the responsibilities of executives to the requirements of a policy, and the continuous comparison of actual with budgeted results, either to secure by individual action the objectives of that policy or to provide a basis for its revision. *See* Figure 3.1.

capital expenditure control

Procedures for authorising and subsequently monitoring capital expenditure. *See* CIMA *Management Accounting Guide No.6.*

capital expenditure proposal/authorisation

A formal request for authority to incur capital expenditure. This is usually supported by the case for expenditure in accordance with capital investment appraisal criteria. .

Levels of authority must be clearly defined and the reporting structure of actual expenditure must be to the equivalent authority levels. *See* CIMA *Management Accounting Guide No.6.*

cash budget

A detailed budget of estimated cash inflows and outflows incorporating both revenue and capital items. In government accounting, budgets for cash expenditure are referred to as cash limits.

control limits

Quantities or values outside which managerial action is triggered. *See* management by exception.

cut-off

A date and procedure for isolating the flow of cash and goods, stock-taking and the related documentation, to ensure that all aspects of a transaction are dealt with in the same financial period.

departmental/functional budget

A budget of income and/or expenditure applicable to a particular function. A function may refer to a department or a process. Functional budgets frequently include:
- production cost budget (based on a forecast of production and plant utilisation);
- marketing cost budget, sales budget;
- personnel budget;
- purchasing budget;
- research and development budget.

enterprise resource planning (ERP)

A software system which is designed to support and automate the business processes of medium and large enterprises. ERP systems are accounting oriented information systems which aid in identifying and planning the enterprise wide resources needed to resource, make, account for and deliver customer orders. Initially developed from MRP II systems, ERP tends to incorporate a number of software developments such as the use of relational databases, object oriented programming and open system portability.

fixed budget

A budget which is normally set prior to the start of an accounting period, and which is not changed in response to subsequent changes in activity or costs/revenues. Fixed budgets are generally used for planning purposes.

flexible budget

A budget which, by recognising different cost behaviour patterns, is designed to change as volume of activity changes.

imposed/top-down budget

A budget allowance which is set without permitting the ultimate budget holder to have the opportunity to participate in the budgeting process.

incremental budgeting

A method of budget setting in which the prior period budget is used as a base for the current budget, which is set by adjusting the prior period budget to take account of any anticipated changes.

kaizen budget

A budget into which is incorporated the expectation of continuous performance improvement throughout the budget period.

line item budget

Traditional form of budget layout showing, line by line, the costs of a cost object analysed by their nature (salaries, occupancy, maintenance etc.).

management by exception

The practice of focusing on activities which require attention and ignoring those which appear to be conforming to expectations.

management control

All of the processes used by managers to ensure that organisational goals are achieved and procedures adhered to, and that the organisation responds appropriately to changes in its environment.

closed loop system

A control system which includes a provision for corrective action, taken on either a *feedforward* or a *feedback* basis.

feedback control

The measurement of differences between planned outputs and actual outputs achieved, and the modification of subsequent action and/or plans to achieve future required results. *See* Figure 5.1.

feedforward control

The forecasting of differences between actual and planned outcomes, and the implementation of action, before the event, to avoid such differences. *See* Figure 5.2.

open loop system

A control system which includes no provision for corrective action to be applied to the sequence of activities.

master budget

The budget into which all subsidiary budgets are consolidated, normally comprising budgeted profit and loss account, budgeted balance sheet and budgeted cash flow statement. These documents, and the supporting subsidary budgets, are used to plan and control activities for the following year.

FIGURE 5.1 A FEEDBACK CONTROL SYSTEM

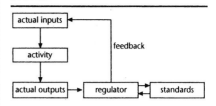

FIGURE 5.2 A FEEDFORWARD CONTROL SYSTEM

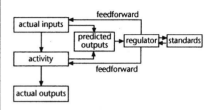

negotiated budget

A budget in which budget allowances are set largely on the basis of negotiations between budget holders and those to whom they report.

noise

Irrelevant or insignificant data which overload a feedback process. The presence of noise can confuse or divert attention from relevant information; efficiency in a system is enhanced as the ratio of information to noise increases.

operating budget

A budget of the revenues and expenses expected in a forthcoming accounting period.

operational control

The management of daily activities in accordance with strategic and tactical plans. *See* Figure 4.12.

participative/bottom-up budgeting

A budgeting system in which all budget holders are given the opportunity to participate in setting their own budgets.

principal budget factor
A factor which will limit the activities of an undertaking and which is often the starting-point in budget preparation. *See* limiting factor (Chapter 4).

priority-based budgeting
A method of budgeting in which budget requests are accompanied by a statement outlining the changes which would occur if the prior period budget were to be increased or decreased by a certain amount or percentage. These changes are prioritised.

relevant range
The activity levels within which assumptions about cost behaviour in breakeven analysis remain valid.

rolling/continuous budget
A budget continuously updated by adding a further accounting period (month or quarter) when the earliest accounting period has expired. Its use is particularly beneficial where future costs and/or activities cannot be forecast accurately. *See* rolling forecast (Chapter 4).

stock control
The systematic regulation of stock levels. Called *inventory control* in the USA. *See* economic order quantity (Chapter 3).

virement
Authority to apply saving under one subhead to meet excesses on others.

zero-based budgeting
A method of budgeting which requires each cost element to be specifically justified, as though the activities to which the budget relates were being undertaken for the first time. Without approval, the budget allowance is zero.

CHAPTER 6

❖

Standard Costing

The final part of this chapter (Figures 6.4 onwards) illustrates calculations of the principal variances. These, for simplicity, assume purchases and consumption to be the same; in practice they may differ, in which case price differences would normally be extracted at the earliest opportunity. Other calculation methods may be used and some variances may be analysed further, as when a material price variance is further analysed by type of material, or by source of supply. The uniform format and simplified data are included to achieve clarity in demonstrating the application of principles.

Marginal costing is used as a convenient vehicle by which to introduce variance analysis. In the examples, ( ) indicates an adverse variance. Favourable or adverse variances may also be identified as (F) or (A) respectively within the various operating statements which are represented.

ex ante

Before the event. An *ex ante* budget, or standard, is set before a period of activity commences, and is based on the best information available at *that time* on expected levels of cost, performance, etc.

ex post

After the event. An ex post budget, or standard, is set after the end of a period of activity, when it can represent the optimum achievable level of performance in the conditions which were experienced. Thus the budget can be flexed, and standards can reflect factors such as unanticipated changes in technol-

ogy and in price levels. This approach may be used in conjunction with sophisticated cost and revenue modelling to determine how far both the plan and the achieved results differed from the performance that would have been expected in the circumstances which were experienced.

standard

A benchmark measurement of resource usage, set in defined conditions. Standards can be set on a number of bases:

(a) on an *ex ante* estimate of expected performance
(b) on an *ex post* estimate of attainable performance
(c) on a prior period level of performance by the same organisation
(d) on the level of performance achieved by comparable organisations
(e) on the level of performance required to meet organisational objectives.

Standards may also be set at attainable levels which assume efficient levels of operation, but which include allowances for normal loss, waste and machine downtime, or at ideal levels, which make no allowance for the above losses, and are only attainable under the most favourable conditions.

standard cost

The planned unit cost of the products, components or services produced in a period. The standard cost may be determined on a number of bases (*see* standard). The main uses of standard costs are in performance measurement, control, stock valuation and in the establishment of selling prices. *See* standard product specification, below.

standard cost card/standard product specification

A document or other record detailing, for each individual product, the standard inputs required for production as well as the standard selling price. Inputs are normally divided into material, labour and overhead categories, and both price and quantity information is shown for each.

standard direct labour cost

The planned average cost of direct labour. *See* standard hour and standard performance.

standard hour or minute

The amount of work achievable, at standard efficiency levels, in an hour or minute.

standard performance–labour

The level of efficiency which appropriately trained, motivated and resourced employees can achieve in the long run.

variance

The difference between a planned, budgeted or standard cost and the actual cost incurred. The same comparisons may be made for revenues.

variance accounting

A method of accounting by means of which planned activities (quantified through budgets and standard costs and revenues) are compared with actual results. Provides information for variance analysis.

variance analysis

The evaluation of performance by means of variances, whose timely reporting should maximise the opportunity for managerial action.

variance, administrative cost

A measurement of the extent of any over- or underspend on administrative costs.

(budgeted cost of administration – actual cost)

variance, budget

The difference, for each cost or revenue element in a budget, between the budgeted amount and the actual cost or revenue. Where flexible budgeting is employed, it is the difference between the flexed budget and the actual value.

variance, direct labour efficiency

Indicates the standard labour cost of any change from the standard level of labour efficiency.

((actual production in standard hours × standard direct labour rate per hour) – (actual direct labour hours worked × standard direct labour rate per hour))

This formula is used where non-productive time (indirect labour) is analysed and controlled as an overhead cost. Where non-productive time is regarded as direct labour, a direct labour efficiency variance and an idle time variance are required.

variance, direct labour mix

Where substitutions between the grades of labour used to operate a process are possible, the mix variance measures the cost of any variation from the standard mix. The variance, for each grade of labour, is based on (i) the change in its weighting within the overall mix, and (ii) whether its unit standard cost is greater or less than the standard weighted average cost of all labour inputs. The labour mix variance is a subdivision of the direct labour efficiency variance.

((actual hours worked – budgeted hours worked for the

output produced) × (standard weighted average cost per hour worked – standard cost per hour worked))

This variance may also be calculated without reference to the relative cost of the various material inputs.

((actual labour hours worked × standard cost per hour worked) – (total labour hours worked in standard proportions × standard cost per labour hour))

The total mix variance is identical under both methods of calculation, whereas the individual input mix variances may be quite different.

It is recommended that the mix variance be calculated by the first method, that is, including in the calculation the relative costs of the inputs.

variance, direct labour rate

Indicates the actual cost of any change from the standard labour rate of remuneration.

((actual hours paid × standard direct labour rate per hour) – (actual hours paid × actual direct labour rate per hour))

variance, direct labour total

Indicates the difference between the standard direct labour cost of the output which has been produced and the actual direct labour cost incurred.

((standard hours produced × standard direct labour rate per hour) – (actual hours paid × actual direct labour rate per hr))

variance, direct material mix

Where substitutions within the mix of materials input to a process are possible, the mix variance measures the cost of any variation from the standard mix. The variance, for each input, is based on (i) the change in its weighting within the overall mix,

and (ii) whether its unit standard cost is greater or less than the standard weighted average cost of all material inputs. A subdivision of the direct material usage variance.

((actual input quantity – budgeted material input quantity for the output produced) × (standard weighted average cost per input unit – standard cost per input unit))

This variance may also be calculated without reference to the relative cost of the various material inputs.

((actual material input × standard cost per unit) – (total actual material input in standard proportions × standard cost per unit))

The total mix variance is identical under both methods of calculation, whereas the individual material input mix variances may be quite different.

It is recommended that the mix variance be calculated by the first method, that is, including in the computation the relative costs of the inputs.

variance, direct material price

The difference between the actual price paid for purchased materials and their standard cost.

((actual quantity of material purchased × standard price) – actual cost of material purchased)

The material price variance may also be calculated at the time of material withdrawal from stores. In this case, the stock accounts are maintained at actual cost, price variances being extracted at the time of material usage rather than of purchase.

((actual material used × standard cost) – actual cost of material used)

variance, direct material total

A measurement of the difference between the standard material cost of the output produced and the actual material cost incurred.

(standard material cost of output produced – actual cost of material purchased)

Where the quantities of material purchased and used are different, the total variance should be calculated as the sum of the usage and price variances.

variance, direct material usage

Measures efficiency in the use of material, by comparing the standard cost of material used with the standard material cost of what has been produced.

((actual production × standard material cost per unit) – (actual material used × standard cost per unit))

The sum of mix and yield variances.

variance, direct material yield

Measures the effect on cost of any difference between the actual material usage and that justified by the output produced.

It is recommended that this variance is only calculated in total, and not for individual material inputs. A subdivision of the direct material usage variance.

((actual material input quantity – budgeted material input quantity for the output produced) × standard weighted average cost per unit of material input)

variance, fixed production overhead capacity

Measures the over- or under-absorption of fixed production overhead costs caused by the actual hours worked differing from the hours originally budgeted to be worked. A subdivision of the fixed production overhead volume variance.

((actual hours worked × standard fixed production overhead absorption rate per hour) – (budgeted hours to be worked × standard fixed production overhead absorption rate per hour))

variance, fixed production overhead efficiency

Measures the over- or under-absorption of fixed production overhead costs caused by actual labour efficiency differing from the standard level of labour efficiency. A subdivision of the fixed production overhead volume variance.

((actual hours worked × standard fixed production overhead absorption rate per hour) – (actual production in standard hours × fixed production overhead absorption rate per hour))

variance, fixed production overhead expenditure

The difference between the fixed production overhead which should have been incurred in the period, and that which was incurred.

(budgeted fixed production overhead – actual fixed production overhead)

variance, fixed production overhead total

The difference between the actual fixed production overhead incurred and the amount absorbed by output produced. This is the sum of the expenditure and volume variances.

((actual production in standard hours × fixed production overhead absorption rate per hour) – actual fixed production overhead)

variance, fixed production overhead volume

A measure of the over- or under-absorption of overhead cost caused by actual production volume differing from that budgeted.

((actual production in standard hours × fixed production overhead absorption rate per hour) – budgeted fixed production overhead)

variance, idle time

The standard labour cost of unproductive paid hours, when production was not possible due to factors such as material unavailability, production planning errors or machine breakdown.

((actual hours paid × standard direct labour rate per hour) – (actual hours worked × standard direct labour rate per hour))

variance, joint

A variance which is caused by both the prices and quantities of inputs differing from the specifications in the original standard. *See* Figure 6.3.

variance, market share

A subdivision of the sales volume contribution variance, applicable when the actual market size of a product or product group is known. It indicates the change in contribution caused by a change in market share.

((sales units representing the budgeted share of the actual market × standard contribution per unit) – (actual sales units × standard contribution per unit))

variance, market size

A subdivision of the sales volume contribution variance, applicable when the actual market size of a product or product group is known. It indicates the change in contribution caused by a change in the size of the market.

(budgeted contribution – (sales units representing the budgeted share of the actual market × standard contribution per unit))

variance, marketing cost

(budgeted marketing cost – actual marketing cost)

Where marketing cost contains both fixed and variable components, separate variances should be calculated.

variance, operational

A classification of variances in which non-standard performance is defined as being that which differs from an *ex post* standard. Operational variances can relate to any element of the standard product specification.

variance, planning

A classification of variances caused by *ex ante* budget allowances being changed to an *ex post* basis. Also known as a revision variance.

variance, sales mix contribution

The change in contribution caused by a change in the mix of the products or services sold.

((actual sales units × budgeted weighted average standard contribution per unit) – (actual sales units × individual standard contribution per unit))

This method of computation highlights the contribution effect, by product, of selling products whose individual standard contributions differ from the budgeted weighted average standard contribution.

The sales mix contribution variance can also be calculated as follows:

((actual sales units – total actual sales units in budgeted proportions) × (standard contribution per unit – budgeted weighted average standard contribution per unit)

This method of computation highlights the contribution effect, by product, of sales deviating from the budgeted proportions. A favourable variance denotes either selling pro-

portionately more of a relatively
high contribution earning product,
or proportionately less of a relatively low contribution product.

variance, sales mix profit

The change in profit caused by a
change in the mix of the products
or services sold.

((actual sales units × budgeted
weighted average standard
profit per unit) – (actual sales
units × individual standard
profit per unit))

This method of computation highlights the profit effect, by product,
of selling products whose individual standard profits differ from the
budgeted weighted average standard profit.

The sales mix profit variance
can also be calculated as follows:

((actual sales units – total actual
sales in budgeted proportions) ×
(standard profit per unit –
budgeted weighted average
standard profit per unit))

This method of computation highlights the profit effect, by product,
of the sales mix deviating from the
budgeted proportions. A favourable
variance denotes either selling proportionately more of a relatively
high profit earning product, or proportionately less of a relatively low
contribution product.

variance, sales price

The change in revenue caused by
the actual selling price differing
from that budgeted.

((actual sales volume × standard
selling price per unit) – actual
sales revenue)

**variance, sales quantity
contribution**

The change in contribution caused
by a difference between actual and
budgeted sales quantities. It is

assumed that the actual sales mix is
in budgeted proportions.

((budgeted sales units ×
budgeted weighted average
standard contribution per unit)
– (total actual sales units ×
budgeted weighted average
standard contribution per unit))

variance, sales quantity profit

The change in profit caused by a
difference between actual and budgeted sales quantities. It is assumed
that the actual sales mix is in budgeted proportions.

((budgeted sales units × budgeted
weighted average standard profit
per unit) – (total actual sales units
× budgeted weighted average
standard profit per unit))

**variance, sales volume
contribution**

The change in contribution caused
by sales volume differing from that
budgeted.

((budgeted sales × standard
contribution per unit) – (actual
sales × standard contribution
per unit))

variance, sales volume profit

The change in profit caused by sales
volume differing from that
budgeted.

((budgeted sales × standard
profit per unit) – (actual sales ×
standard profit per unit))

variance, sales volume revenue

The change in sales revenue caused
by actual sales volume differing
from that budgeted.

((budgeted sales units × standard selling price per unit) –
(actual sales units × standard
selling price per unit))

variance, total profit

The difference between the profit as
per the original budget and the
actual profit achieved. The total

profit variance is the sum of all of the subsidiary variances which have been produced.

(budgeted profit – actual profit)

variance, variable production overhead efficiency

Measures the difference between the variable overhead cost budget flexed on actual labour hours, and the variable overhead cost absorbed by output produced.

((actual hours worked × standard variable production overhead absorption rate per hour) – (actual production in standard hours × variable absorption rate per hour))

If variable production overheads vary with output produced this variance will not be relevant, since the flexed budget variable overhead and the variable overhead absorbed will always be identical, and the variance zero.

variance, variable production overhead expenditure

Measures the difference between the actual variable production over-head costs and those in a budget flexed on labour hours

(actual cost incurred – (actual hours worked × standard variable production overhead absorption rate per hour))

If variable production overheads vary with output, rather than with hours worked, the variance would be calculated as follows:

(actual cost incurred – (output produced × variable production overhead rate per unit produced))

variance, variable production overhead total

The difference between the amount of variable production overhead which has been absorbed by output, and the actual cost. Where variable production overhead varies with output, this is identical to the variable production overhead expenditure variance.

(actual cost incurred – (actual production in standard hours × variable production overhead absorption rate per hour))

FIGURE 6.1 CHART OF VARIANCES (MARGINAL COSTING PRINCIPLES). SEE DEFINITIONS

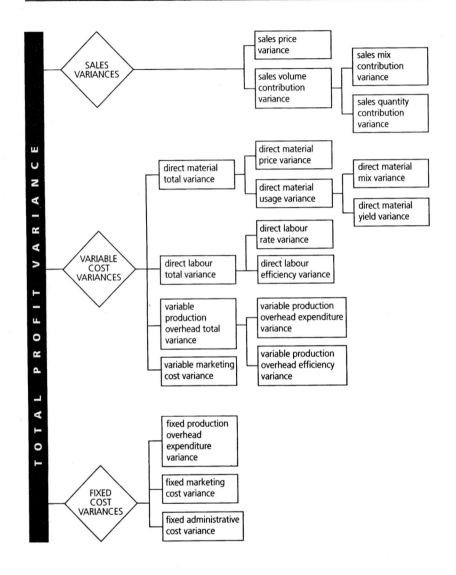

**FIGURE 6.2 CHART OF VARIANCES (ABSORPTION COSTING PRINCIPLES).
SEE DEFINITIONS**

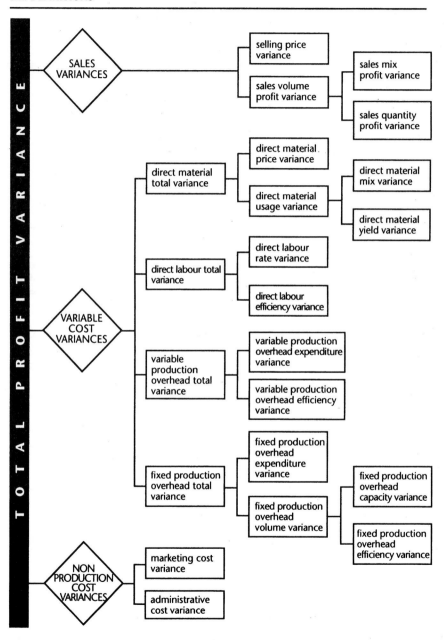

FIGURE 6.3 JOINT VARIANCES

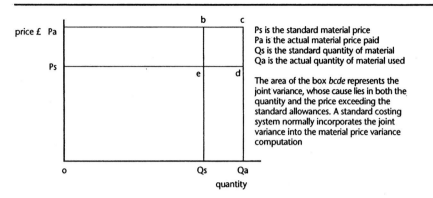

Ps is the standard material price
Pa is the actual material price paid
Qs is the standard quantity of material
Qa is the actual quantity of material used

The area of the box *bcde* represents the joint variance, whose cause lies in both the quantity and the price exceeding the standard allowances. A standard costing system normally incorporates the joint variance into the material price variance computation

In figures 6.4–6.11 adverse variances are identified by brackets.

FIGURE 6.4 OPERATING STATEMENT WITH FLEXED BUDGET

Period ....

	Standard per unit	Fixed Budget*	Flexed Budget	Actual	Flexible Budget Variances
No. of units made and sold	1	1,000	1,100	1,100	
	£	£	£	£	£
Sales	70.00	70,000	77,000	82,500	5,500
Direct material 1 kg @ £15	15.00	15,000	16,500	17,000	(500)
Direct labour 1 hr @ £10	10.00	10,000	11,000	11,250	(250)
Variable production overhead:					
1 hr @ £2.50	2.50	2,500	2,750	3,050	(300)
Total variable costs	27.50	27,500	30,250	31,300	
Contribution	42.50	42,500	46,750	51,200	
Fixed production overhead 1 hr @ £5	5.00	5,000	5,000	5,300	(300)
Gross profit	37.50	37,500	41,750	45,900	
Fixed marketing cost		12,500	12,500	12,950	(450)
Fixed administrative cost		13,000	13,000	13,550	(550)
		25,500	25,500	26,500	
Operating profit		12,000	16,250	19,400	3,150

£4,250
Sales volume
contribution
variance

£3,150
Price, usage and
expenditure
variances

Fixed budget profit – actual profit =

£7,400
Total profit variance

FIGURE 6.5 STANDARD COSTING VARIANCES (MARGINAL COSTING BASIS)

Note: 1,200 kg of materials were purchased and used; 1,250 labour hours were worked

		£
Sales volume contribution		
(Budgeted sales × standard contribution per unit) – (Actual sales × standard contribution per unit)		
(1,000 × £42.50) – (1,100 × £42.50)	=	4,250
Sales price		
(Actual sales volume × standard selling price per unit) – Actual sales revenue		
(1,100 × £70) – £82,500	=	5,500
Direct material price		
(Actual quantity of material purchased × standard price) – Actual cost of material purchased (1,200 × £15) – £17,000	=	1,000
Direct material usage		
(Actual production × standard material cost per unit) – (Actual material used × standard cost per unit) (1,100 × £15) – (1,200 × £15)	=	(1,500)
Direct labour rate		
(Actual hours paid × standard direct labour rate per hour) – (Actual hours paid × actual direct labour rate per hour) (1,250 × £10) – £11,250	=	1,250
Direct labour efficiency		
(Actual production in standard hours × standard direct labour rate per hour) – (Actual direct labour hours worked × standard direct labour rate per hour) (1,100 × £10) – (1,250 × £10)	=	(1,500)
Variable production overhead expenditure		
Actual cost incurred – (Actual hours worked × standard variable production overhead absorption rate per hour) £3,050 – (1,250 × £2.50)	=	75
Variable production overhead efficiency		
(Actual hours worked × standard variable production overhead absorption rate per hour) – (Actual production in standard hours × variable production overhead absorption rate per hour) (1,250 × £2.50) – (1,100 × £2.50)	=	(375)
Fixed production overhead expenditure		
Budgeted fixed production overhead – Actual fixed production overhead £5,000 – £5,300	=	(300)
NOTE: Expenditure variances relating to all fixed costs can be derived from a Flexed Budget v. Actual comparison.		

ADDITIONAL VARIANCES FOR STANDARD ABSORPTION COSTING

Sales volume profit		
(Budgeted sales × standard profit per unit) – (Actual sales × standard profit per unit) (1,000 × £37.50) – (1,100 × £37.50)	=	3,750
Fixed production overhead volume		
(Actual production in standard hours × standard fixed production overhead absorption rate per hour) – Budgeted fixed production overhead (1,100 × £5) – £5,000	=	500

The fixed production overhead volume variance could be subdivided as follows:

Fixed production overhead efficiency		
(Actual hours worked × standard fixed production overhead absorption rate per hour) – (Actual production in standard hours × standard fixed production overhead absorption rate per hour) (1,250 × £5) – (1,100 × £5)	=	(£750)
Fixed production overhead capacity		
(Actual hours worked × standard fixed production overhead absorption rate per hour) – (Budgeted hours to be worked × standard fixed production overhead absorption rate per hour) (1,250 × £5) – (1,000 × £5)	=	£1,250

FIGURE 6.6 OPERATING STATEMENT – STANDARD MARGINAL COSTING

Period ....

	£	£	£	£
Budgeted sales				70,000
Budgeted variable cost of sales				27,500
Budgeted contribution				42,500
Sales volume contribution variance				4,250
Budgeted contribution from actual sales				46,750
Variances		(F)	(A)	
Sales price		5,500	–	
Direct material usage		–	(1,500)	
Direct material price		1,000	–	
Direct labour efficiency		–	(1,500)	
Direct labour rate		1,250	–	
Variable overhead efficiency			(375)	
Variable overhead expenditure		75		
		7,825	(3,375)	4,450
Actual contribution				51,200
Fixed costs				

	£		£	
	Budget		Expenditure variance	
Production	5,000		(300)	
Marketing	12,500		(450)	
Administration	13,000		(550)	
	30,500		(1,300)	31,800
Actual profit				19,400

FIGURE 6.7 OPERATING STATEMENT – STANDARD ABSORPTION COSTING

Period ....

	£	£	£
Budgeted sales			70,000
Budgeted cost of sales			32,500
			37,500
Budgeted marketing cost		12,500	
Budgeted administration cost		13,000	25,500
Budgeted profit			12,000
Sales volume profit variance			3,750
Budgeted profit from actual sales			15,750
Variances	(F)	(A)	
Sales price	5,500	–	
Marketing cost	–	(450)	
Direct material usage	–	(1,500)	
Direct material price	1,000	–	
Direct labour efficiency	–	(1,500)	
Direct labour rate	1,250	–	
Variable overhead efficiency	–	(375)	
Variable overhead expenditure	75	–	
Fixed overhead volume	500	–	
Fixed overhead expenditure	–	(300)	
Fixed administrative cost	–	(550)	
	8,325	(4,675)	3,650
Actual profit			19,400

FIGURE 6.8 WORKED EXAMPLE OF DIRECT MATERIALS YIELD AND MIX VARIANCES

1. Initial data: Materials Y and Z are mixed in the proportions 60% and 40% respectively and a standard loss of 4.5% is set. Standard and actual costs for a period show:

	Standard			Actual		
	Quantity in mix	Unit cost	Total cost	Quantity in mix	Unit cost	Total cost
	Kg	£/kg	£	Kg	£/kg	£
Material Y	30,000	3.20	96,000	24,000	3.40	81,600
Material Z	20,000	2.40	48,000	21,000	2.00	42,000
Input	50,000		144,000	45,000		123,600
4.5% Standard loss	2,250					
Output	47,750			42,000		

2. The results of the calculations and the relationships between the variances are as follows:

| Direct material total variance | £3,060 |

| Direct material price variance | £3,600 | | Direct material usage variance | £ (540) |

| Direct material mix variance | £2,400 | | Direct material yield variance | £(2,940) |

Direct material price variances   £
(Actual quantity of material purchased × standard price) - (Actual cost of material purchased)
Y (24,000 × £3.20) – (24,000 × £3.40)   = (4,800)
Z (21,000 × £2.00) – (21,000 × £2.40)   = 8,400
                                                                                                                  3,600

Direct material usage variances
(Actual production × standard material cost per unit) – (Actual material used
× standard material cost per unit)
Y ((42,000 × 0.6) ÷ 0.955) × £3.20 – (24,000 × £3.20)   = 7,640
Z ((42,000 × 0.4) ÷ 0.955) × £2.40 – (21,000 × £2.40)   = (8,180)
                                                                                                                  (540)

Direct material mix variance
(Actual input quantity - budgeted material input quantity for the output produced)
x (standard weighted average cost per input unit - standard cost per input unit)
Y (24,000 – 26,387) × (£2.88 – £3.20)   = 764
Z (21,000 – 17,592) × (£2.88 – £2.40)   = 1,636
                                                                                                                  = 2,400

Direct material yield variance
(Actual material input quantity – budgeted material input quantity for the output
produced) × Standard weighted average cost per unit of material input
(45,000 – 43,979) × £2.88   = (2,940)

Unlike mix and price variances, the yield variances for each individual material in a mix is of no managerial interest

NOTE: The material mix variance may also be calculated without reference to the relative costs of the inputs to the mix, as follows:

Direct material mix variance
(Actual material input quantity x standard cost per unit) – (Total actual material input in standard proportions × standard cost per unit)
Y (24,000 × £3.20) – (27,000 × £3.20)   = 9,600
Z (21,000 × £2.40) – (18,000 × £2.40)   = (7,200)
                                                                                                                  2,400

FIGURE 6.9 WORKED EXAMPLE OF SALES PROFIT VARIANCES

Budgeted sales data
Product F 3,000 units with standard profit of £2.00 per unit
Product G 4,000 units with standard profit of £2.50 per unit
Product H 3,000 units with standard profit of £3.00 per unit
Weighted average standard profit is £2.50 per unit

Actual sales data
Product F 3,000 units
Product G 3,000 units
Product H 6,000 units

	£
Sales volume profit variance	
(Budgeted sales × standard profit per unit) – (Actual sales x standard profit per unit)	
[(3,000 × £2.0) + (4,000 × £2.5) + (3,000 × £3.0)] –	
[(3,000 × £2.00) + (3,000 × £2.50) + (6,000 × £3.0)]	6,500

	£
Sales quantity profit variance	
(Budgeted sales units × budgeted weighted average standard profit per unit) –	
(Total actual sales units × budgeted weighted average standard profit per unit)	
(10,000 × £2.50) – (12,000 × £2.50)	5,000

	£
Sales mix profit variance	
(Actual sales units × budgeted weighted average standard profit per unit) –	
(Actual sales units × individual standard profit per unit)	
F (3,000 × £2.50) – (3,000 × £2.00)	(1,500)
G (3,000 × £2.50) – (3,000 × £2.50)	–
H (6,000 × £2.50) – (6,000 × £3.00)	3,000
	1,500

An alternative method of calculating the sales mix profit variance is as follows:

	Actual sales units	Actual sales units in budgeted proportions	Difference units	Standard unit profit	Budgeted weighted average standard unit profit	Variance £
F	3,000	3,600	– 600	£2.0	£2.50	300
G	3,000	4,800	– 1,800	£2.5	£2.50	–
H	6,000	3,600	+ 2,400	£3.0	£2.50	1,200
						1,500

The results of the calculations and their relationships are as follows:

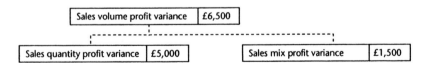

Sales volume profit variance	£6,500

| Sales quantity profit variance | £5,000 | | Sales mix profit variance | £1,500 |

Note 1 Where unit quantities are not available or relevant, units would be replaced by turnover, and profit per unit replaced by profit to sales ratios.
Note 2 If a marginal costing system was in operation, the following variances would be calculated with respect to sales:
  i   Sales volume contribution variance
  ii   Sales quantity contribution variance
  iii Sales mix contribution variance
  These variances would be calculated in an identical manner to the above sales profit variances, although based on standard unit contribution, rather than standard unit profit, information.

FIGURE 6.10 WORKED EXAMPLE OF MARKET VARIANCES

The budgeted sales of 1,000 units in Figure 6.4 represented a 20% share of the estimated market of 5,000 units. Actual sales of 1,100 units gave rise to a sales volume contribution variance of £4,250. To judge sales performance, the actual market, found to be 6,500 units, is taken into account.

				£
(a)	Budget representing 20% of	5,000 unit market 1,000 units @ £42.50	=	42,500
(b)	20% of actual market of	6,500 units 1,300 units @ £42.50	=	55,250
(c)	Actual sales representing 16.923% of	1,100 units @£42.50 6,500 units	=	46,750
(a-b)	Market size variance			12,750
(b-c)	Market share variance			(8,500)
(a-c)	Sales volume contribution variance			4,250

FIGURE 6.11 WORKED EXAMPLE OF PLANNING AND OPERATIONAL VARIANCES

Before the start of the period
◆ the standard purchase price of material was set at £2.00 per kg

During the period
◆ the budgeted quantity of material specified for the output in the period: 20,000 kg
◆ the actual material purchased and used: 21,000kg
◆ the actual purchase price paid: £2.80, due to an unforeseen occurrence which led to a material shortage

At the period end a price of £3.00 was agreed to have been an efficient buying price in the period. The standard costing system shows a direct material total variance of £18,000 made up of:
  material usage variance (£2,000)
  material price variance (£16,800)

Management wishes to distinguish between controllable and uncontrollable effects on performance.

Variance calculations
  Planning price variance
    Originally budgeted material purchase quantity × (*ex post* efficient standard purchase price per kg – budgeted standard purchase price per kg)
    20,000 × (£3.00 – £2.00)   (20,000)
  Operational usage variance
    (Actual production × *ex post* efficient standard material cost/unit) – (actual material used x *ex post* efficient standard material cost per unit)
    (20,000 × £3.00) – (21,000 × £3.00)   (£3,000)
  Operational price variance
    Actual material purchase quantity × (*ex post* efficient standard purchase price per kg – actual purchase price per kg)
    21,000 × (£3.00 – £2.80)   £4,200

Continued

Operating statement

	£	£
MATERIAL		
Standard cost of output		
(20,000 kg × £2)		40,000
Planning price variance		
(20,000 kg × £1)		(20,000)
Revised standard cost of output		60,000
Operational usage variance		
(1,000 kg × £3)	(3,000)	
Operational price variance		
(21,000 kg × £0.20)	4,200	1,200
Actual cost of material used		58,800

The planning price variance indicates that the original standard purchase price was not achievable. The operational usage variance indicates the standard cost (*ex post*) of the excess usage of material which took place in the period.

The operational price variance indicates the cost saving which has been achieved by purchasing material at a price lower than the *ex post* standard.

CHAPTER 7

❖

Performance Measures

accounting rate of return

$$\frac{\text{Average annual profit from an investment} \times 100}{\text{Average investment}}$$

Sometimes used in investment appraisal, and a form of return on capital employed. Unlike net present value and internal rate of return, the ratio is based on profits, not cash flows. Exclusive use of this ratio is not recommended.

asset cover

$$\frac{\text{Net tangible assets before deducting overdraft and other borrowings}}{\text{Total borrowings including overdraft}}$$

Indicates the safety of lenders' money.

asset value per share

$$\frac{\text{Total assets less liabilities}}{\text{Number of issued equity shares}}$$

Shows the value of assets per share, to assist with investment and disinvestment decisions, usually for the benefit of equity shareholders.

bad debts ratio

$$\frac{\text{Bad debts} \times 100}{\text{Turnover on credit}}$$

Numerator and denominator should be moving annual totals. Indicates the significance of bad debts as a proportion of credit sales.

$$\frac{\text{Bad debts} \times 100}{\text{Total debtors at a point in time}}$$

Indicates the significance of bad debts as a proportion of debtors.

capacity ratios

Measures of performance in the use of capacity. The more commonly used capacity levels are:
♦ full capacity – output (expressed in standard hours) that could be achieved if sales orders, supplies and workforce were available for all installed workplaces.
♦ practical capacity – full capacity less an allowance for known unavoidable volume losses.
♦ budgeted capacity – standard hours planned for the period, taking into account budgeted sales, supplies, workforce availability and efficiency expected.
♦ normal capacity.

On the following given data, the related ratios are set out below:

Full capacity standard hours	100
Practical capacity standard hours	95
Budgeted capacity (budgeted input hours, 90 at 90 per cent efficiency)	81
Actual input hours	85
Standard hours produced	68

Idle capacity ratio:

$$\frac{(\text{Practical capacity} - \text{budgeted capacity}) \times 100}{\text{Practical capacity}}$$

$$= \frac{(95 - 81) \times 100}{95} = 15\%$$

Indicates the budgeted shortfall in capacity as a proportion of practical capacity.

Production volume ratio:

$$\frac{\text{Standard hours produced} \times 100}{\text{Budgeted capacity}}$$

$$= \frac{68 \times 100}{81} = 84\%$$

Shows the actual output as a proportion of budgeted output.

Efficiency ratio:

$$\frac{\text{Standard hours produced} \times 100}{\text{Actual hours}}$$

$$= \frac{68 \times 100}{85} = 80\%$$

Measures the relationship between output produced and productive time taken, which may be measured in either direct labour or machine hours, as appropriate.

capital turnover

$$\frac{\text{Turnover for the year}}{\text{Average capital employed in year}}$$

Expresses the number of times the capital is turned over in the year and the turnover generated by each £1 of capital employed.

compound interest

Interest which is calculated over successive periods based on the principal plus accrued interest. *See* simple interest

The future value of an investment, over whose period interest is compounded, can be found by using the following formula:

$S = X(1 + r)^n$

Where:

S = Future value in year n

X = Initial investment or value at year 0

r = Annual rate of return expressed as a fraction

n = Number of years

Example:

Investment of £400 (X)

Time period of 4 years (n)

Annual interest is 8% (r)

$S = £400(1 + 0.08)^4 = £544.2$

contribution per unit of limiting factor ratio

$$\frac{\text{Product/service contribution}}{\text{Product/service usage of units of limiting factor}}$$

Used in marginal costing to measure the contribution to fixed overhead and profit generated by the use of each unit of limiting factor. This is used to rank alternative uses of the limiting factor.

contribution to sales ratio

$$\frac{\text{Revenue minus all variable costs} \times 100}{\text{Revenue}}$$

Of particular use in product profit planning and as a means of ranking alternative products.

creditor days ratio

$$\frac{\text{Average trade creditors}}{\text{Average daily purchases on credit terms}}$$

Indicates the average time taken, in calendar days, to pay for supplies received on credit.

Adjustment is needed if the ratio is materially distorted by VAT or other taxes.

debtor days ratio

$$\frac{\text{Average trade debtors}}{\text{Average daily turnover on credit terms}}$$

Indicates the average time taken, in calendar days, to receive payment from credit customers.

Adjustment is needed if the ratio is materially distorted by VAT or other taxes.

dividend cover

$$\frac{\text{Earnings per share}}{\text{Dividend per share}}$$

Indicates the number of times the profits attributable to the equity shareholders cover the net dividends payable for the period.

dividend payout ratio

$$\frac{\text{Ordinary dividends for the year}}{\text{Earnings attributable to the ordinary shareholders}}$$

Shows the proportion of earnings which are distributed to the ordinary shareholders by way of dividends.

dividend per share

Total amounts declared as dividends per share. The dividend per share actually paid in respect of a financial year. Special rules apply if equity shares are issued during the year.

dividend yield

$$\frac{\text{Dividend per share net of any taxes deducted at source} \times 100}{\text{Market price per share}}$$

Shows as a percentage the post-tax dividend return on market value offered by the shares.

earnings per share (EPS)

$$\frac{\text{Attributable equity profit for the period}}{\text{Number of equity shares ranking for dividend}}$$

Special rules apply if equity shares are issued during the year. FRS 3 defines earnings per share as follows:

'The profit in pence attributable to each equity share, based on the profit (or in the case of a group the consolidated profit) of the period after tax, minority interests and extraordinary items and after deducting preference dividends and other appropriations in respect of preference shares, divided by the number of equity shares in issue and ranking for dividend in respect of the period.

earnings yield

$$\frac{\text{Earnings per share} \times 100}{\text{Market price of a share}}$$

Indicates as a percentage the total amount earned in respect of each equity share in issue, in relation to the market price of a share. The earnings yield computation can

also be based on the aggregate earnings and the market value of the equity capital.

economy

The acquisition of resources of appropriate quantity and quality at minimum cost. *See* Figure 7.1.

effectiveness

The utilisation of resources such that the output of the activity achieves the desired result. *See* Figure 7.1.

efficiency

The achievement of either (i) maximum useful output from the resources devoted to an activity, or (ii) the required output from the minimum resource input. *See* Figure 7.1.

FIGURE 7.1 ECONOMY, EFFECTIVENESS AND EFFICIENCY

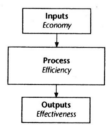

fixed asset turnover

$$\frac{\text{Turnover for the year}}{\text{Average net book value of fixed assets}}$$

Indicates the turnover generated by each £1 of fixed assets, or the number of times fixed assets are turned over in the year.

forfaiting

The purchase of financial instruments such as bills of exchange or letters of credit on a non-recourse basis by a forfaiter, who deducts interest (in the form of a discount) at an agreed rate for the period covered by the notes. The forfaiter assumes the responsibility for claiming the debt from the importer (buyer) who initially accepted the financial instrument drawn by the seller of the goods. Traditionally, forfaiting is fixed-rate, medium-term (one- to five-year) finance.

gearing/leverage

This relates to financial gearing, which is the relationship between a company's borrowings, which includes both prior charge capital and long-term debt, and its shareholders' funds (ordinary share capital plus reserves). Gearing calculations can be made in a number of ways, and may be based on capital values or on earnings/interest relationships. Overdrafts and interest paid thereon may also be included:

$$\frac{\text{Profit before interest and tax}}{\text{Profit before tax}}$$

Shows the effect of interest on the operating profit.

$$\frac{\text{Profit before interest and tax}}{\text{Interest expense}}$$

Shows the number of times that profit will cover interest expense.

$$\frac{\text{Total long-term debt}}{\text{Shareholders' funds plus long-term debt}}$$

Shows the proportion of long-term financing which is being supplied by debt.

$$\frac{\text{Total long-term debt}}{\text{Total assets}}$$

A measure of the capacity to redeem debt obligations by the sale of assets.

$$\frac{\text{Operating cashflows – taxation paid – returns on investment and servicing of finance}}{\text{Repayments of debt due within one year}}$$

Measures ability to redeem debt.

A company with a high proportion of prior charge capital to shareholders' funds is high geared, and is low geared if the reverse situation applies.

gross profit percentage

$$\frac{(\text{Sales – cost of sales}) \times 100}{\text{Sales for the period}}$$

Used to gain an insight into the relationship between production/purchasing costs and sales revenues.

interest cover

$$\frac{\text{Profit before gross interest and tax}}{\text{Gross interest payable}}$$

Used by lenders to determine vulnerability of interest payments to a drop in profit.

length of order book

$$\frac{\text{Sales value of orders outstanding}}{\text{Sales value of production per day/week/month}}$$

The sales value of production may be based on planned, current or available capacity production.

liquidity ratios

Relate to working capital and indicate the ability to meet liabilities from assets available.

The most commonly used are:
acid test/quick ratio

$$\frac{\text{Current assets – stock at end of period}}{\text{Current liabilities at end of period}}$$

Indicates the ability to pay creditors in the short term.
current ratio:

$$\frac{\text{Current assets at end of period}}{\text{Current liabilities at end of period}}$$

An overall measure of liquidity.

margin of safety ratio

$$\frac{(\text{Forecast turnover} - \text{breakeven turnover}) \times 100}{\text{Forecast turnover}}$$

Indicates the percentage by which forecast turnover exceeds or falls short of that required to break even.

non-financial performance measures

Measures of performance based on non-financial information which may originate in and be used by operating departments to monitor and control their activities without any accounting input.

Non-financial performance measures may give a more timely indication of the levels of performance achieved than do financial ratios, and may be less susceptible to distortion by factors such as uncontrollable variations in the effect of market forces on operations.

Examples of non-financial performance measures:

Area assessed	Performance measure
Service quality	Number of complaints
	Proportion of repeat bookings
	Customer waiting time
	On-time deliveries
Production performance	Set-up times
	Number of suppliers
	Days' inventory in hand
	Output per employee
	Material yield percentage
	Schedule adherence
	Proportion of output requiring rework
	Manufacturing lead times

Area assessed	Performance measure
Marketing effectiveness	Trend in market share
	Sales volume growth
	Customer visits per salesperson
	Client contact hours per salesperson
	Sales volume forecast v. actual
	Number of customers
	Customer survey response information
Personnel	Number of complaints received
	Staff turnover
	Days lost through absenteeism
	Days lost through accidents/sickness
	Training time per employee

The values expected may vary significantly between industries/sectors.

normal capacity

A measure of the long-run average level of capacity that may be expected. This is often used in setting the budgeted fixed overhead absorption rate (giving it stability over time, although budgeted fixed overhead volume variances are generally produced as a consequence).

price/earnings ratio (P/E ratio)

$$\frac{\text{Market price per share}}{\text{Earnings per share}}$$

Shows the number of years it would take to recoup an equity investment from its share of the attributable equity profit. The P/E ratio values the shares of the company as a multiple of current or of prospective earnings, and thus gives a market view of the quality of the underlying earnings.

probability

The likelihood of an event or a state of nature occurring, being measured in a range from 0 (no possibility) to 1 (certainty).

profit per employee

$$\frac{\text{Profit for the year before interest and tax}}{\text{Average number of employees}}$$

An indication of the effectiveness of the employment of staff. When there are full- and part-time employees, full-time equivalents should be used. *See* sales per employee.

profit to turnover ratio (profit margin %)

$$\frac{\text{Profit before interest and tax} \times 100}{\text{Turnover}}$$

A key profitability ratio. If the numerator is not multiplied by 100 it shows the profit generated by each £1 turnover.

profitability index

$$\frac{\text{Present value of cash inflows}}{\text{Initial investment}}$$

Used in investment appraisal. Rep-resents the net present value of each £1 invested in a project.

ratio pyramid

The analysis of a primary ratio into mathematically linked secondary ratios. For example:

Primary ratio

(a) $\dfrac{\text{Profit}}{\text{Capital employed}}$

Secondary ratio

(b) $\dfrac{\text{Profit}}{\text{Turnover}}$ (c) $\dfrac{\text{Turnover}}{\text{Capital employed}}$

Ratio a = b × c. Ratios b and c can be analysed by further ratios if desired. The pyramid continues with further analysis of the secondary ratios. *See* Figures 7.2, 7.3 and 7.4.

return on capital employed (ROCE)

$$\frac{\text{Profit before interest and tax} \times 100}{\text{Average capital employed}}$$

FIGURE 7.2 RATIO PYRAMID FOR A MANUFACTURER

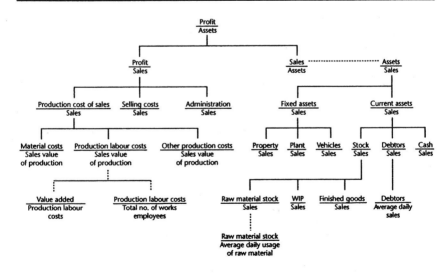

Indicates the productivity of capital employed.

The denominator is normally calculated as the average of the capital employed at the beginning and end of year. Problems of seasonality, new capital introduced or other factors may necessitate taking the average of a number of periods within the year. The ROCE is known as the primary ratio in a ratio pyramid. *See* capital employed (Chapter 9).

return on equity

$$\frac{\text{Profit after interest and tax}}{\text{Ordinary share capital plus reserves}}$$

A form of return on capital employed which measures the return to the owners on their investment in a company. The return is measured as the residual profit after all charges and appropriations other than to the ordinary shareholders have been made, and the equity is ordinary share capital plus reserves.

FIGURE 7.3 RATIO PYRAMID FOR A RETAILER

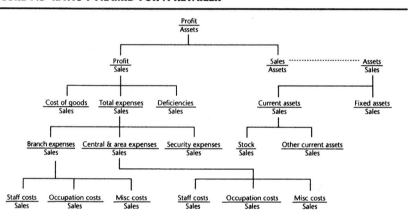

FIGURE 7.4 RATIO PYRAMID FOR SERVICES

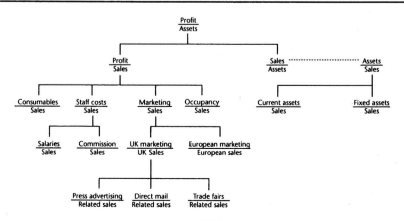

return on investment (ROI)

$$\frac{\text{Profit before interest and tax}}{\text{Operations management capital employed}}$$

A form of return on capital employed, which compares income with the operational assets used to generate that income.

Profit is taken before tax and interest because tax is an appropriation of profit made from the use of the investment, and the introduction of interest charges introduces the effect of financing decisions into an appraisal of operating performance.

sales per employee

$$\frac{\text{Turnover for the year}}{\text{Average number of employees}}$$

An indicator of labour productivity. *See* profit per employee.

simple interest

Interest which is calculated over successive periods based only on the principal. *See* compound interest.

stock turnover

number of days' stock

$$\frac{\text{Stock value}}{\text{Average daily cost of sales in period}}$$

Number of days stocks at the forecast or most recent usage rate. Can be applied to finished goods, raw material and work in progress by using appropriate numerators.

number of weeks' stock – internal

The efficiency of stock utilisation is indicated by the following internally used ratios:

$$\frac{\text{Finished goods stock}}{\text{Average weekly despatches}}$$

$$\frac{\text{Raw material stock}}{\text{Average weekly raw material usage}}$$

$$\frac{\text{Work in progress}}{\text{Average weekly production}}$$

The above ratios are calculated using values; quantities can be used where appropriate.

number of weeks' stock – external

$$\frac{\text{Total stocks}}{\text{Average weekly turnover or cost of sales}}$$

Financial analysts who only have access to published accounts often use the total closing stock value in relation to the year's cost of sales.

❖

CHAPTER 8

Financial Accounting Statements and Documents

account sales
A statement rendered to a consignor of merchandise by the consignee, giving particulars of sales, the quantity remaining unsold, gross proceeds, expenses incurred, consignee's commission, and net amount due to the consignor.

age analysis of debtors
The amount owed by debtors, classified by age of debt.

annual report and accounts
A set of statements which may comprise a management report (in the case of companies, the directors' report), and the financial statements of an entity.

In the case of companies these accounts are drawn up for a period which is called the *accounting reference period*, the last day of which is known as the *accounting reference date*.

appropriation account
In trading and not-for-profit entities, record of how the profit/loss or surplus/deficit has been allocated to distributions/reserves/funds.

audit report
The formal document in which an auditor expresses an opinion as to whether the financial statements of an entity:
◆ show a true and fair view of:
   – its position at a given date; and
   – the results of its operations for the accounting period ended on that date

◆ have been properly prepared in accordance with the relevant statutory requirements
or
any report by an auditor in accordance with the terms of appointment.

Where the auditors have no reservations concerning the application by a company of appropriate accounting policies, that compliance with all legislation, accounting standards and regulation has taken place, and that all information relevant to the proper understanding of the financial statements has been produced, they will issue an *unqualified audit report*. Where they have reservations about any of the above they will issue a *qualified audit report*, stating their reservations.

balance sheet
A statement of the financial position of an entity at a given date disclosing the assets, liabilities and accumulated funds such as shareholders' contributions and reserves, prepared to give a true and fair view of the financial state of the entity at that date. *See* Figure 8.4

bank reconciliation
A detailed statement reconciling, at a given date, the cash balance in an entity's cash book with that reported in a bank statement.

An example is given below.

EXAMPLE:
Bank Reconciliation Statement
Cash book balance

	£	£
Cash book balance o/d		(1,205)
Bank charges not in cash book	(110)	
Dividends collected by the bank, not in cash book	113	3
Updated cash book balance*		(1,202)
Cheques drawn, not presented to bank	4,363	
Cheques received, not yet credited by bank	(1,061)	3,302
Bank statement balance		2,100

* The balance sheet will show a bank overdraft of £1,202, which is the true position at the date of the reconciliation, after corrections by journal entry.

bank statement
A record, sent by a bank to its customer, listing transactions since the date of the previous statement.

bill
noun – popular name for an invoice.
verb – to render an account, i.e. to send an invoice.

bill of exchange
A negotiable instrument, drawn by one party on another, for example by a supplier of goods on a customer, who by accepting (signing) the bill, acknowledges the debt, which may be payable immediately (a sight draft) or at some future date (a time draft). The holder of the bill can thereafter use an accepted time draft to pay a debt to a third party, or can discount it to raise cash.

bill of lading
A document prepared by a consignor by which a carrier acknowledges the receipt of goods and which serves as a document of title to the goods consigned.

bill of materials
A specification of the materials and parts required to make a product.

bill payable
A bill of exchange or promissory note payable.

bill receivable
A bill of exchange or promissory note receivable.

cash-flow statement
A statement listing the inflows and outflows of cash and cash equivalents for a period, classified under the following standard headings:
◆ operating activities;
◆ returns on investment and servicing of finance;
◆ taxation;
◆ investing activities; and
◆ financing. (FRS 1)
See Figure 8.5

cheque
A bill of exchange drawn on a banker payable on demand (Bills of Exchange Act 1882).

cheque register
A control record of cheques issued or received.

coin analysis
The quantities and denominations of banknotes and coins required to pay employees on a payroll.

control account
A ledger account which collects the sum of the postings into the individual accounts which it controls. The balance on the control account should equal the sum of the balances on the individual accounts, which are maintained as subsidiary records.

credit note
A document prepared by a seller notifying the purchaser that the account is being reduced by a stated amount, e.g. because of an allowance, return of goods or cancellation.

credit report

Information about an individual or entity relevant to a decision to grant credit.

current account

A record of transactions between two parties, e.g. between a bank and its customer or a branch and head office.

debit note

A document prepared by a purchaser notifying the seller that the account is being reduced by a stated amount, e.g. because of an allowance, return of goods or cancellation.

delivery note

A document containing details of the quantity and specifications of accompanying goods. A signed copy of the delivery note often acts as proof of delivery. The delivery note may also be referred to as a despatch note, a carrier's note or a consignment note. An advice note contains similar information, but is sent to inform a third party of delivery.

departmental accounts

Revenue and expenditure statements for departments of an entity. Usually take the form of a trading and profit and loss account for each department or operating accounts for service departments.

direct debit

A direct claim on an individual or organisation by a creditor, and paid by the individual's or organisation's bank on each occasion. Variations in period claims are admissible.

financial statements

Summaries of accounts, whether to internal or external parties, to provide information for interested parties. The most common financial statements are:

◆ trading and profit and loss account;

◆ profit and loss appropriation account;

◆ balance sheet;

◆ cash-flow statement;

◆ report of the auditors;

◆ statement of total recognised gains and losses;

◆ reconciliation of movements in shareholders' funds.

fixed assets register

A record of individual tangible fixed assets.

float/petty cash

A small cash balance maintained to facilitate low-value cash transactions. Records of these transactions should be maintained as evidence of expenditure, and periodically a float or petty cash balance will be replenished to a predetermined level.

goods received note

A record of goods at the point of receipt.

group accounts

The financial statements of a group, prepared usually by consolidation (FRS 2).

horizontal group

The situation where two or more undertakings are controlled by a common parent, such as a private individual, who is not subject to the requirements of the Companies Act or FRS 2. There is therefore no legal or professional mechanism which can be used to require the preparation of consolidated financial statements. *See* group accounts.

impersonal account

Any account other than a personal account, being classified as:

◆ a real account, in which property is recorded; or

◆ a nominal account, in which income, expenses and capital are recorded.

See account, personal account.

income and expenditure account

A financial statement for not-for-profit entities such as clubs, associations and charities. It shows the surplus or deficit, being the excess of income over expenditure or vice versa, for a period and is drawn up on the same accruals basis as a profit and loss account.

income statement

See trading, profit and loss account.

interest charged

The cost of borrowing money, expressed as an absolute amount, or as a % interest rate. *See* annual percentage rate, nominal interest rate, real interest rate (Chapter 10).

invoice

A document prepared by a supplier showing the description, quantities, prices and values of goods delivered or services rendered.

To the supplier this is a sales invoice; to the purchaser the same document is a purchase invoice.

invoice register

A list of purchase invoices recording date of receipt of the invoice, the supplier, invoice value and to whom the invoice has been passed, to ensure that all invoices received are processed by the accounting system.

journal

A record of original entry, into which transactions are normally transferred from source documents. The journal may be subdivided into:

♦ sales journal/day book for credit sales;
♦ purchases journal/day book for credit purchases;
♦ cash book for cash receipts and payments;
♦ the journal proper for transactions which could not appropriately be recorded in any of the other journals.

ledger

A collection of accounts, maintained by transfers from the books of original entry. The ledger may be subdivided as follows:

♦ sales ledger/debtors ledger contains the personal accounts of all customers;
♦ purchases ledger/creditors ledger contains all the personal accounts of suppliers;
♦ private ledger contains accounts relating to the proprietor's interest in the business such as capital and drawings;
♦ general ledger/nominal ledger contains all other accounts relating to assets, expenses, revenue and liabilities.

letter of credit

A document issued by a bank on behalf of a customer authorising a person to draw money to a specified amount from its branches or correspondents, usually in another country, when the conditions set out in the document have been met.

materials returned note

A record of the return to stores of unused material.

materials/stores requisition

A document, raised by a production/user department, authorising the issue from stores of a specified quantity of material. Any surplus material issued should be returned to stores accompanied by a materials returned note.

materials transfer note

A record of any transfers of material between stores, cost centres or cost units.

operating statement

A regular report for management of actual costs and revenues, as appropriate. Usually compares actual with budget and shows variances. *See*

Chapter 6, Figures 6.4, 6.6 and 6.7.

out-of-date cheque

A cheque which has not been presented to the bank on which it is drawn for payment within a reasonable time of its date (six months in the UK) and which may therefore be dishonoured by the bank without any breach of the banker–customer contract.

paid cheque

A cheque which has been honoured by the bank on which it was drawn, and bears evidence of payment on its face.

petty cash account

A record of relatively small cash receipts and payments, the balance representing the cash in the control of an individual, usually dealt with under an imprest system.

petty cash voucher

A document supporting payments under a petty cash system.

plan comptable

A uniformly structured and detailed bookkeeping system, compliance with which is required of companies in France.

prime entry, books of

A first record of transactions, such as sales or purchases, from which either detail or totals, as appropriate, are transferred to the ledgers.

pro-forma invoice

An invoice sent to the purchaser in advance of goods, for completion of business formalities (usually for payment before despatch of goods).

promissory note

A negotiable instrument, governed by the Bills of Exchange Act 1992, in the form of an unconditional written and signed promise by one person to another to pay a certain sum of money on demand or at a future time.

purchase order

A written order for goods or services specifying quantities, prices, delivery dates and contract terms.

purchase requisition

An internal instruction to a buying office to purchase goods or services, stating their quantity and description and generating a purchase order.

receipts and payments account

A report of cash transactions during a period. It is used in place of an income and expenditure account when it is not considered appropriate to distinguish between capital and revenue transactions or to include accruals.

reconciliation of movements in shareholders' funds

A financial statement which brings together the performance of the period, as shown in the statement of total recognised gains and losses, with all the other changes in shareholders' funds in the period, including capital contributed by or repaid to shareholders (FRS 3). *See* Figure 8.2

sales order

An acknowledgement by a supplier of a purchase order. It may contain terms which override those of the purchaser.

segmental reporting

The inclusion in accounts of analysis of turnover, profits and net assets by class of business and by geographical segments.

Figure 8.8 illustrates a segmental report for published accounts in a shareholders' report (Companies Act 1985 and SSAP 25).

sight draft

A bill of exchange payable on presentation. Three days of grace are allowed for payment.

source document

A document upon which details of transactions or accounting events are recorded, and from which information is extracted to be subsequently entered into the internal accounting system of an organisation, e.g. sales invoice, credit note.

standing order

An order for the supply of goods or services, as need or opportunity arises, usually limited by a stated maximum.

In banking: a customer's instruction to pay a stated amount to another person on specified dates.

statement of account

A list of sums due, usually relating to unpaid invoices, items paid on account but not offset against particular invoices, credit notes, debit notes and discounts.

statement of affairs

A statement, usually prepared by a receiver, in a prescribed form, showing the estimated financial position of a debtor or of a company which may be unable to meet its debts.

It contains a summary of the debtor's assets and liabilities. The assets are shown at their estimated realisable values. The various classes of creditors, such as preferential, secured, partly secured and unsecured, are shown separately.

statement of total recognised gains and losses

A financial statement which includes the profit or loss for the period together with all other movements on reserves reflecting recognised gains and losses attributable to shareholders (FRS 3). *See* Figure 8.3.

suspense account

An account in which debits or credits are held temporarily until sufficient information is available for them to be posted to the correct accounts.

tangible fixed asset statement

A summary of the opening and closing balances for tangible fixed assets (fixed assets having a physical identity) and acquisitions, disposals and depreciation in the period. *See* Figure 8.7.

trading, profit and loss account

An account which shows the gross profit or loss generated by an entity for a period (trading account), and after adding other income and deducting various expenses shows the profit or loss of the business (the profit and loss account). Figure 8.1 shows a typical format which meets the requirements of the Companies Acts 1985/1989. Reference may be made to the four alternative formats in Schedule IV of the Companies Act 1985.

Some small entities combine the two accounts.

trial balance

A list of account balances in a double-entry accounting system. If the records have been correctly maintained, the sum of the debit balances will equal the sum of the credit balances, although certain errors such as the omission of a transaction or erroneous entries will not be disclosed by a trial balance.

variance, direct labour yield

Measures the effect on cost of any difference between the actual labour hours worked and the hours justified by output produced. It is recommended that this variance is only calculated in total, and not for individual labour grades. It is a subdivision of the direct labour efficiency variance.

((actual labour hours worked – budgeted labour hours for the output produced) – (standard weighted average cost per hour))

voucher
Documentary evidence supporting an accounting entry.

FIGURE 8.1 GROUP PROFIT AND LOSS ACCOUNT FOR THE FINANCIAL YEAR ENDED 31 MARCH 2001

	£m
Turnover	
Continuing operations	3,694.8
Discontinued operations	–
	3,694.8
Net operating costs	3,589.2
Operating profit	105.6
Discontinued operations	–
Profit on ordinary activities before interest	105.6
Net interest payable	2.4
Profit on ordinary activities before taxation	103.2
Taxation	29.7
Profit for the financial year	73.5
Dividends	24.6
Retained profit for the financial year	48.9
Earnings per ordinary share	
on profit for the financial year	20.5p
on continuing operations	20.5p

FIGURE 8.2 RECONCILIATION OF MOVEMENTS IN SHAREHOLDERS' FUNDS

	£m
Retained profit for the financial year	48.9
Goodwill	(9.9)
Other recognised gains and losses for the year	4.3
Net additions to shareholders' funds	43.3
Shareholders' funds at beginning of year	258.5
Shareholders' funds at end of year	301.8

FIGURE 8.3 STATEMENT OF TOTAL RECOGNISED GAINS AND LOSSES FOR THE YEAR ENDED 31 MARCH 2001

	£m
Retained profit for the financial year	48.9
Revaluation adjustment	5.0
Currency translation difference on foreign currency net investment	(0.7)
	53.2

FIGURE 8.4 GROUP BALANCE SHEET AS AT 31 MARCH 2001

	£m	£m
Fixed assets		
Tangible assets	264.3	
Intangible assets	12.0	
		276.3
Current assets		
Stocks		220.2
Debtors – *due within one year*		234.6
– *pension prepayment*		76.5
Cash at bank and in hand		101.7
		633.0
Creditors: amounts due within one year		
Bank loans and overdrafts		74.7
Other		482.1
Net current assets		76.2
Total assets less current liabilities		352.5
Creditors: amounts due after more than one year		
Taxation		0.6
Finance debt		14.7
Provision for liabilities and charges		
Deferred taxation		25.5
Other		9.9
Net assets		301.8
Capital and reserves		
Called-up share capital		106.8
Reserves		
Revaluation reserve		7.2
Other reserves		4.2
Profit and loss account		183.6
Equity shareholders' funds	236.7	
Non-equity shareholders' funds	65.1	
		301.8

FIGURE 8.5 GROUP CASH-FLOW STATEMENT FOR THE YEAR ENDED 31 MARCH 2001

	£m
Net cash inflow from operating activities	162.9
Returns on investment and servicing of finance	
Interest received	2.1
Interest paid	(3.9)
Dividends paid	(23.7)
Net cash outflow from returns on investments and servicing of finance	(25.5)
Tax paid	(16.2)
Investing activities	
Businesses acquired	(9.9) — Goodwill
Purchase of fixed assets	(80.1)
Sale of fixed assets	4.2
Net cash outflow from investing activities	(85.8)
Net cash inflow before financing	35.4
Financing	
Finance leases	(0.9)
Loans	7.5
Net cash inflow/(outflow) from financing	6.6
Increase in cash and cash equivalents	42.0

FIGURE 8.6 EXAMPLE NOTE TO PROFIT AND LOSS ACCOUNT

Net Operating Cost

	2001 Discontinued £m	2001 Continuing £m	2000 Continuing £m	2000 Discontinued £m	2000 Total £m
Goods for resale and consumables	–	3,003.3	2,773.5	50.4	2,823.9
Other operating charges	–	191.4	189.9	22.2	212.1
Employment costs	–	350.4	330.6	1.5	332.1
Depreciation	–	41.1	38.4	0.3	38.7
Amortisation	–	3.0	3.0	–	3.0
		3,589.2	3,335.4	74.4	3,409.8
Other operating charges include					
Hire charges	–	10.8			10.5
Rent of properties	–	119.4			115.5
Remuneration of auditors	–	0.9			0.6

The auditors also received £0.8m in respect of non-audit services during the year.

FIGURE 8.7 EXAMPLE NOTE TO BALANCE SHEET

Tangible Fixed Assets

	Freehold £m	Long Leasehold £m	Short Leasehold £m	Plant and Equipment £m	Total £m
Cost or valuation at					
1 April 2000	40.2	4.8	66.0	295.8	406.8
Additions	16.8	4.2	5.4	53.7	80.1
Businesses acquired	–	–	–	1.5	1.5
Transfers	–	–	(1.2)	1.2	–
Disposals	(1.2)	–	(4.8)	(31.8)	(37.8)
At 31 March 2001	55.8	9.0	65.4	320.4	450.6
Depreciation					
at 1 April 2000	0.9	–	23.4	150.6	174.9
Charge for the year	0.6	0.3	3.6	36.6	41.1
Businesses acquired	–	–	–	0.3	0.3
Transfers	–	–	–	–	–
Disposals	–	–	(2.7)	(27.3)	(30.0)
At 31 March 2001	1.5	0.3	24.3	160.2	186.3
Net book value at					
31 March 2001	54.3	8.7	41.1	160.2	264.3
Net book value at					
31 March 2000	39.3	4.8	42.6	145.2	231.9

Short leasehold properties have less than 50 years unexpired at 31 March 2001.

At 31 March 2001 the net book value of fixed assets acquired under finance leases amounted to £9.3m and the depreciation charge for the year thereon was £3.3m.

FIGURE 8.8 SEGMENTAL ANALYSIS

	Turnover		Profit		Net assets	
	£m	£m	£m	£m	£m	£m
	2001	2000	2001	2000	2001	2000
Plastics	2,727.9	2,506.5	72.0	62.7	143.7	115.8
Internal sales	(239.4)	(202.2)	–	–	–	–
	2,488.5	2,304.3	72.0	62.7	143.7	115.8
Electronics	1,206.3	1,127.1	33.6	33.3	233.4	243.6
	3,694.8	3,431.4	105.6	96.0	377.1	359.4
Discontinued operations	–	72.9	–	1.8	–	–
	3,694.8	3,504.3	105.6	97.8	377.1	359.4
Interest payable	–	–	(2.4)	(5.7)		
	3,694.8	3,504.3	103.2	92.1		

		2001	2000
Gross capital employed		377.1	359.4
Unallocated financial items		75.3	96.6
Net assets		301.8	262.8

Overseas turnover was not significant.

The results of acquisition during the year were not material.

CHAPTER 9

❖

Financial Accounts

accounting reference period
The period for which a company makes up its accounts. This period is normally, although not necessarily, 12 months. Also used for taxation where it represents the period upon whose adjusted profits corporation tax is based.

accrued expenses
Charges which are brought into the financial statements at the end of a period because, although goods and services have been provided, they have not yet been charged for by the suppliers. For example, electricity, invoiced in arrears, generally requires accrual at the end of each accounting period.

administrative expenses
The cost of management, secretarial, accounting and other services which cannot be related to the separate production, marketing or research and development functions.

advance corporation tax (ACT)
Formerly an amount payable in advance of the final tax liability, arising whenever a dividend or other qualifying distribution is made by a company. (Withdrawn 5-4-99). *See* shadow ACT.

amortisation
The systematic write-off of the cost of an intangible asset

assets
Rights or other access to future economic benefits controlled by an entity as a result of past transactions or events (FRS 5).

intangible assets
Non-financial fixed assets that do not have physical substance but are

identifiable and are controlled by the entity through custody or legal rights (FRS 10).

tangible assets
Assets having a physical identity, e.g. plant and machinery.

attributable profit (on contracts)
That part of the total profit currently estimated to arise over the duration of a contract (after allowing for likely increases in cost so far as not recoverable under the terms of the contract) which fairly reflects the profit attributable to that part of the work performed at the accounting date.

(There can be no attributable profit until the outcome of the contract can be assessed with reasonable certainty.) (SSAP 9)

bad debt
A debt which is or is considered to be uncollectable and is, therefore, written off either as a charge to the profit and loss account or against an existing doubtful debt provision. *See* doubtful debts provision.

bank charge
An amount charged by a bank to its customers for services provided, e.g. for servicing customer accounts or arranging foreign currency transactions or letters of credit, but excluding interest.

bank overdraft
Borrowings from a bank on current account, repayable on demand.

The maximum permissible overdraft is normally agreed with the bank prior to the facility being made available, and interest, calculated on a daily basis, is charged on the amount borrowed, and not on the agreed maximum borrowing facility.

bonus/scrip issue

The capitalisation of the reserves of a company by the issue of additional shares to existing shareholders, in proportion to their holdings. Such shares are normally fully paid-up with no cash called for from the shareholders. *See* rights issue.

capital commitment

The estimated amount of capital expenditure:
- ◆ contracted for but not yet provided for; *and*
- ◆ authorised by the directors but not yet contracted for.

capital employed

The funds used by an entity for its operations. This can be expressed in various ways depending upon the purpose of the computation, e.g. for operations evaluation, capital employed may be defined as the total value of non-current assets plus working capital, whereas for investor evaluation, owners' capital plus reserves may be used.

capital expenditure

The cost of acquiring, producing or enhancing fixed assets. *See* revenue expenditure.

capital redemption reserve

An account required to prevent a reduction in capital, where a company purchases or redeems its own shares out of distributable profits.

commodity contract

A contract that provides for settlement by receipt or delivery of a commodity (FRS 13).

constructive obligation

An obligation that derives from an entity's actions where:
(a) by an established pattern of past practice, published policies or a sufficiently specific current

statement, the entity has indicated to other parties that it will accept certain responsibilities; and
(b) as a result, the entity has created a valid expectation on the part of those other parties that it will discharge those responsibilities.
(FRS 12)

contingent asset

A possible asset that arises from past events and whose existence will be confirmed only by the occurrence of one or more uncertain future events not wholly within the entity's control (FRS 12).

contingent liability

(a) A possible obligation that arises from past events and whose existence will be confirmed only by the occurrence of one or more uncertain future events not wholly within the entity's control; or
(b) A present obligation that arises from past events but is not recognised because:
  (i) it is not probable that a transfer of economic benefits will be required to settle the obligation; or
  (ii) the amount of the obligation cannot be measured with sufficient reliability.
(FRS 12)

control in the context of an asset

The ability to obtain the future economic benefits relating to an asset and to restrict the access of others to these benefits (FRS 5).

control of another entity

The ability to direct the financial and operating policies of that entity with a view to gaining economic benefit from its activities (FRS 5).

control procedures

Those policies and procedures in addition to the control environment which are established to achieve the entity's specific objectives. They include in particular procedures designed to prevent or detect and correct errors (SAS 300).

convertible loan stock

A loan which gives the holder the right to convert to other securities, normally ordinary shares, at a predetermined price/rate and time.

corporation tax

Tax chargeable on companies resident in the UK or trading in the UK through a branch or agency as well as on certain unincorporated associations.

cost of sales

The sum of variable cost of sales plus factory overhead attributable to the sales.

In management accounts this may be referred to as production cost of sales or cost of goods sold.

creditor

A person or an entity to whom money is owed as a consequence of the receipt of goods or services in advance of payment. *See* short-term debtors and creditors.

current asset

Cash or other assets, e.g. stock, debtors and short-term investments, held for conversion into cash in the normal course of trading.

current liabilities

Liabilities which fall due for payment within one year. They include that part of long-term loans due for repayment within one year.

current tax

The amount of tax estimated to be payable or recoverable in respect of the taxable profit or loss for a period, along with adjustments to estimates in respect of previous periods. (FRS 16)

date of acquisition

The date on which control of an acquired entity passes to the acquirer. This is the date from which the acquired entity is accounted for by the acquirer as a subsidiary undertaking under FRS 2 *Accounting for Subsidiary Undertakings* (FRS 7).

debenture

The written acknowledgement of a debt by a company, usually given under its seal, and normally containing provisions as to payment of interest and the terms of repayment of principal. A debenture may be secured on some or all of the assets of the company or its subsidiaries.

debtor

A person or an entity owing money. *See* short-term debtors and creditors

deferred expenditure

Expenditure not charged against income in an accounting period but carried forward as a current asset to be charged in a subsequent period, e.g. in certain circumstances development expenditure may be deferred to the extent that its recovery can reasonably be regarded as assured (SSAP 13).

deferred taxation

Taxation attributable to timing differences.

Timing differences are differences between profits or losses as computed for taxation purposes and results as stated in financial statements, which result from the inclusion of items of income and expenditure in taxation computations in periods different from those in which they are included in financial statements.

Timing differences originate in one period and are capable of reversal in one or more subsequent periods (SSAP 15).

depreciation

The measure of the cost or revalued amount of the economic benefits of the tangible fixed asset that have been consumed during the period.

Consumption includes wearing out, using up or other reduction in the useful economic life of a tangible fixed asset whether arising from use, effluxion of time or obsolescence through either changes in technology or demand for the goods and services produced by the asset (FRS 15).

deprival value

Basis for asset valuation based on the maximum amount which an organisation would be willing to pay rather than forgo the asset.

Deprival value
lower of
Replacement Cost   Recoverable Amount
higher of
Realisable Value   Value in Use

development cost

The cost of use of scientific or technical knowledge in order to produce new or substantially improved materials, devices, products or services; to install new processes or systems prior to the commencement of commercial production or commercial applications; or to improve substantially those already produced or installed (SSAP 13).

distribution cost

The cost of warehousing saleable products and delivering them to customers.

dividend

An amount payable to shareholders from profits or other distributable reserves. Dividends are normally paid in cash, but *scrip dividends*,

paid by the issue of additional shares, are permissible. Listed companies normally pay two dividends per year, an interim dividend, based on interim profits reported during the accounting period, and a final dividend, based on the final audited accounts and approved at the Annual General Meeting.

doubtful debts provision

An amount charged against profit and deducted from debtors to allow for the estimated non-recovery of a proportion of the debts. *See* bad debt.

entity (legal)

A body corporate, partnership or unincorporated association carrying on a trade or business with or without a view to profit. The reference to carrying on a trade or business means a trade or business of its own, and not just part of the trades or businesses of entities that have interests in it (FRS 9).

equity

The issued ordinary share capital plus reserves, statutory and otherwise, which represent the investment in a company by the ordinary shareholders.

equity share capital

A company's issued share capital less capital which carries preferential rights. Equity share capital normally comprises ordinary shares.

exceptional items

Material items which derive from events or transactions that fall within the ordinary activities of the reporting entity individually or, if a similar type, in aggregate and which need to be disclosed separately by virtue of their size or incidence if the financial statements are to give a true and fair view (FRS 3).

extraordinary items

Material items possessing a high

degree of abnormality which arise from events or transactions that fall outside the ordinary activities of the reporting entity and which are not expected to recur. They do not include exceptional items, nor do they include prior period items merely because they relate to a prior period (FRS 3).

factored goods
Goods purchased for resale.

finished goods
Manufactured goods ready for sale or despatch.

fixed asset
Any asset, tangible or intangible, acquired for retention by an entity for the purpose of providing a service to the business, and not held for resale in the normal course of trading.

fixed charge
A form of protection given to secured creditors relating to specific assets of a company. The charge grants the holder the right of enforcement against the identified asset (in the event of default on repayment) so that the creditor may realise the asset to meet the debt owed. Fixed charges rank first in order of priority in receivership or liquidation.

floating charge
A form of protection given to secured creditors which relates to assets of the company which are changing in nature. Often current assets like stock or debtors are the subject of this type of charge. In the event of default on repayment the chargeholder may take steps to enforce the charge so that it crystallises and becomes attached to the current assets to which it relates. Floating charges rank after certain other prior claims in receivership or liquidation.

franked investment income
The total of dividends received plus their associated tax credit.

franked payments
The total of dividends paid plus their associated tax credit.

fungible assets
Assets which are substantially indistinguishable one from another, e.g. investments. The Companies Act allows for stocks and fungible assets to be valued in the balance sheet using FIFO, or LIFO, or a weighted average price, or any other similar method. However, the use of LIFO is not acceptable for the use in the UK for the calculation of profits for tax purposes (SSAP 9).

identifiable assets and liabilities
The assets and liabilities of an entity that are capable of being disposed of or settled separately, without disposing of a business of the entity (FRS 10).

impairment
A reduction in the recoverable amount of a fixed asset or goodwill below its carrying value (FRS 11).

income generating unit
A group of assets, liabilities and associated goodwill that generates income that is largely independent of the reporting entity's other income streams. The assets and liabilities include those directly involved in generating the income and an appropriate portion of those used to generate more than one income stream (FRS 11).

intangible assets
Non-financial fixed assets that do not have physical substance but are identifiable and are controlled by the entity through custody or legal rights (FRS 10).

internal control system
The control environment and

control procedures. It includes all the policies and procedures (internal controls) adopted by the directors and management of an entity to assist in achieving their objectives of ensuring, as far as practicable, the orderly and efficient conduct of a business, including adherence to internal policies, the safeguarding of assets, the prevention and detection of fraud and error, the accuracy and completeness of the accounting records, and the timely preparation of reliable financial information (SAS 300). *See* control environment (Chapter 2), control procedures.

investment
Any application of funds which is intended to provide a return by way of interest, dividend or capital appreciation.

issue costs
The costs that are incurred directly in connection with the issue of a capital instrument, that is, those costs that would not have been incurred had the specific instruments in question not been issued (FRS 4).

joint control
A reporting entity jointly controls a venture with one or more other entities if none of the entities alone can control that entity but all together can do so and decisions on financial and operating policy essential to the activities, economic performance and financial position of that venture require each venturer's consent (FRS 9).

joint venture
An entity in which the reporting entity holds an interest on a long-term basis and is jointly controlled by the reporting entity and one or more other venturers under a contractual arrangment (FRS 9).

key management
Those persons in senior positions having authority or responsibility for directing or controlling the major activities and resources of the reporting entity (FRS 8).

legal obligation
An obligation that derives from:
(a) a contract (through its explicit or implicit terms)
(b) legislation
(c) other operation of law.
(FRS 12)

liabilities
An entity's obligations to transfer economic benefits as a result of past transactions or events (FRS 5).

liability method
A method of computing deferred tax by calculating it at the rate of tax that it is estimated will apply when the timing differences reverse.

Under the liability method deferred tax not provided for is calculated at the expected long-term tax rate (SSAP 15).

liquid assets
Cash, and other assets readily convertible into cash, e.g. short-term investment.

loan capital
Debentures and other long-term loans to a business.

mainstream corporation tax
Formerly the balance of corporation tax due after deducting ACT. *See* advance corporation tax. Withdrawn 5.4.99.

marketing cost
The cost of researching potential markets and promoting a product or service.

minority interest
Nominal value of shares held in a subsidiary undertaking by members other than the parent company or

its nominees plus the appropriate portion of the accumulated reserves, including share premium account.

net assets

The excess of book value of assets over liabilities, including loan capital.

This is equivalent to *net worth*, which is used to describe the paid-up share capital and reserves.

net book value/written-down value

The historical cost of an asset less any accumulated depreciation or other provision for diminution in value, e.g. reduction to net realisable value, or asset value which has been revalued downwards to reflect market conditions.

non-current assets

See fixed asset.

non-equity shares

Shares possessing any of the following characteristics:

(a) any of the rights of the shares to receive payments (whether in respect of dividends, in respect of redemption or otherwise) are for a limited amount that is not calculated by reference to the company's assets or profits or the dividends on any class of equity share;

(b) any of their rights to participate in a surplus in a winding-up are limited to a specific amount that is not calculated by reference to the company's assets or profits and such limitation had a commercial effect in practice at the time the shares were issued or, if later, at the time the limitation was introduced;

(c) the shares were redeemable either according to their terms, or because the holder, or any

party other than the issuer, can require their redemption (FRS 4).

obligating event

An event that creates a legal or constructive obligation that results in an entity having no realistic alternative to settling that obligation (FRS 12).

obsolescence

The loss of value of a fixed asset due to advances in technology or changes in market conditions for its product.

onerous contract

A contract in which unavoidable costs of meeting the obligations under it exceed the economic benefits expected to be received under it (FRS 12).

participating dividend

A dividend (or part of a dividend) on a non-equity share that, in accordance with the company's memorandum and articles of association, is always equivalent to a fixed multiple of the dividend payable on an equity share (FRS 4).

payables

See creditor.

post balance sheet events

Favourable and unfavourable events which occur between the balance sheet date and the date on which the financial statements are approved by the board of directors, or equivalent in other organisations.

They are classified as adjusting events and non-adjusting events (SSAP 17).

adjusting events

Post balance sheet events which provide additional evidence of conditions existing at the balance sheet date. They include events which, because of statutory or conventional requirements, are reflected in the financial statements (SSAP 17).

Financial statements should be

changed to show the effect of material adjusting events. *See* non-adjusting events.

non-adjusting events

Post balance sheet events which concern conditions which did not exist at the balance sheet date (SSAP 17).

Where non-adjusting events are material, disclosure is required if non-disclosure would affect the ability of the users of financial statements to reach a proper understanding of the financial position, although the financial statements themselves are not adjusted. *See* adjusting events, above.

pre-acquisition profits/losses

The profits or losses of a subsidiary undertaking, attributable to a period prior to its acquisition by a parent company. Such profits are not available for distribution as dividends by the parent company unless the underlying value of the subsidiary undertaking is at least equal to its net carrying value in the books of the parent company.

preferred creditors

Creditors entitled to full satisfaction of their claims in insolvency before other claims are met.

prepayments

Expenditure on goods or services for future benefit which is to be charged to future operations, e.g. rentals paid in advance. These amounts are included in current assets.

prior charge capital

Capital which has a right to the receipt of interest or of preference dividends in precedence to any claim on distributable earnings on the part of the ordinary shareholders. On winding up, the claims of holders of prior charge capital also rank before those of ordinary shareholders.

prior period adjustments

Material adjustments applicable to prior periods arising from changes in accounting policies or from the correction of fundamental errors. They do not include normal recurring adjustments or correction of accounting estimates made in prior periods (FRS 3).

profit retained for the year

Non-distributed profit retained as a distributable reserve.

provisions for liabilities and charges

Amounts retained as reasonably necessary to cover any liability or loss which is either likely or certain to be incurred but uncertain as to amount or as to the date on which it will arise (Companies Act).

purchased goodwill

The difference between the cost of an acquired entity and the aggregate of the fair value of that entity's identifiable assets and liabilities.

Positive goodwill arises when the acquisition cost exceeds the aggregate fair values of the identifiable assets and liabilities.

Negative goodwill arises when the aggregate fair values of the identifiable assets and liabilities of the entity exceed the acquisition cost (FRS 10).

raw material

Goods purchased for incorporation into products for sale.

receivables

See debtor.

recoverable amount

The higher of net realisable value and value in use (FRS 10).

research cost, applied

The cost of original or critical investigation undertaken in order to gain new scientific or technical knowledge and directed towards a specific practical aim or objective (SSAP 13).

research cost, pure or basic

The cost of experimental or theoretical work undertaken primarily to acquire new scientific or technical knowledge and understanding, not primarily directed towards any specific practical aim or application (SSAP 13).

reserves

Retained profits or surpluses. In a not-for-profit entity these are described as accumulated funds. Reserves may be distributable (revenue reserves) or non-distributable (capital reserves).

restructuring

A programme that is planned and controlled by management, and materially changes either:

(a) the scope of a business undertaken by an entity; or

(b) the manner in which that business is conducted.

(FRS 12)

retention money or payments withheld

An agreed proportion of a contract price withheld for a specified period after contract completion as security for fulfilment of obligations.

returns

Goods returned by a customer to the supplier, due to factors such as incorrect quality, specification, quantity or damage, or where the original supply was on a 'sale or return' basis.

revenue expenditure

Expenditure on the manufacture of goods, the provision of services or on the general conduct of the entity, which is charged to the profit and loss account in the accounting period of sale. This includes repairs and depreciation of fixed assets as distinct from the provision of these assets. *See* capital expenditure.

rights issue

The raising of new capital by giving existing shareholders the right to subscribe to new shares or debentures in proportion to their current holdings. These shares are usually issued at a discount to market price. A shareholder not wishing to take up a rights issue may sell the rights. *See* bonus issue.

secured creditors

Creditors whose claims are wholly or partly secured on the assets of a business.

selling cost

Cost incurred in securing orders, usually including salaries, commissions and travelling expenses.

shadow ACT

A system which commenced on 6-4-99 to allow relief for surplus ACT which has accumulated at 5-4-99. *See* advance corporation tax.

share

A fixed identifiable unit of capital which has a fixed nominal or face value, which may be quite different from the market value of the share.

convertible share

Non-equity share such as a preference share, carrying rights to convert into equity shares on predetermined terms.

cumulative preference shares

Shares which entitle the holders to a fixed rate of dividend, and the right to have any arrears of dividend paid out of future profits with priority over any distribution of profits to the holders of ordinary share capital.

deferred/founders' shares

A special class of shares ranking for dividend after preference and ordinary shares.

non-voting shares
Shares which carry no voting rights.

ordinary shares
Shares which entitle the holders to the remaining divisible profits (and, in a liquidation, the assets) after prior interests, e.g. creditors and prior charge capital, have been satisfied.

participating preference shares
Shares which entitle the holder to a fixed dividend and, in addition, to the right to participate in any surplus profits after payment of agreed levels of dividends to ordinary shareholders have been made.

preference shares
Shares carrying a fixed rate of dividend, the holders of which, subject to the conditions of issue, have a prior claim to any company profits available for distribution.

Preference shareholders may also have a prior claim to the repayment of capital in the event of winding up.

redeemable shares
Shares which are issued on terms which may require them to be bought back by the issuer at some future date, either at the discretion of the issuer or of the holder. Redemption must comply with the conditions of the Companies Act 1985.

share capital
authorised/nominal/registered share capital
The type, class, number and amount of the shares which a company may issue, as empowered by its memorandum of association.

called-up share capital
The amount which the company has required shareholders to pay on the shares issued.

issued/subscribed share capital
The type, class, number and amount of the shares held by shareholders.

paid-up share capital
The amount which shareholders are deemed to have paid on the shares issued and called up.

uncalled share capital
The amount of the nominal value of a share which is unpaid and has not been called up by the company.

unissued share capital
The amount of the share capital authorised but not yet issued.

share option scheme
An arrangement which gives employees the opportunity to acquire new shares in a company on favourable terms.

share premium
The excess received, either in cash or other consideration, over the nominal value of the shares issued.

shareholders' funds
The aggregate of called-up share capital and all reserves, excluding minority interest (FRS 4).

short-term debtors and creditors
Financial assets and financial liabilities that meet all of the following criteria:
(a) they would be included under one of the following balance sheet headings if the entity was preparing its financial statements in accordance with Schedule 4 to the Companies Act 1985:
(i) debtors;
(ii) prepayments and accrued income;
(iii) creditors: amounts falling due within one year, other than items that would be included under the heading 'debenture loans' and 'bank loans and overdrafts' sub-headings;

(iv) provisions for liabilities and charges; or

(v) accruals and deferred income;

(b) they mature or become payable within 12 months of the balance sheet date; and

(c) they are not a derivative financial instrument.

(FRS 13).

sinking fund
Money put aside periodically to settle a liability or replace an asset. The money is invested to produce a required sum at an appropriate time.

staff costs
The costs of employment which include gross pay, paid holidays and employer's contributions to national insurance, pension schemes, sickness benefit schemes and other benefits, e.g. protective clothing and canteen subsidies.

stock (capital)
An amount of fully paid-up capital, any part of which can be transferred, e.g. a block of £1,000 of stock out of a total holding of £15,000.

stock (goods)
Goods or inventory held, comprising:
◆ goods or other assets purchased for resale;
◆ consumable stores;
◆ raw materials and components purchased for incorporation into products for sale;
◆ products and services, in intermediate stages of completion (work in progress);
◆ long-term contract balances;
◆ finished goods (SSAP 9).

subordinated debt
Debt that ranks below other debt under the terms of the agreement between the borrower and the lender.

tax credit
The tax credit given under UK tax legislation to the recipient of a dividend from a UK company.
The credit is given to acknowledge that income out of which the dividend has been paid has already been charged to tax, rather than because any withholding tax has been deducted at source. The tax credit may discharge or reduce the recipient's liability to tax on the dividend. Non-taxpayers may or may not be able to recover the tax credit.
(FRS 16)

taxable profit or loss
The profit or loss for the period, determined in accordance with the rules established by the tax authorities, upon which taxes are assessed.
(FRS 16)

tests of control
Tests performed to obtain audit evidence about the effective operation of the accounting and internal control systems – that is, that properly designed controls identified in the preliminary assessment (of control risk) exist in fact and have operated effectively throughout the relevant period (SAS 300).

total assets
The total net book value of all assets.

trade creditors
Money owed to suppliers for goods and services. Other money owed, including employers' national insurance and taxation, is to be shown under other creditors.

turnover/sales
Amounts derived from the provision of goods and services falling within the company's ordinary activities, after deduction of returns, trade discounts, value

added tax, and any other taxes based on the amounts so derived (Companies Act 1985). Also called *revenue*.

unfranked investment income
Amounts received by a company net of basic rate tax, e.g. patent royalties.

value in use
The present value of the future cash flows obtainable as a result of an asset's continued use, including those resulting from its ultimate disposal (FRS 10).

variable cost of sales
The sum of direct materials, direct wages, variable production overhead, and variable selling and distribution overhead. *See* Figure 3.6.

wasting asset
A fixed asset which is consumed or exhausted in the process of earning income, e.g. a mine or quarry.

withholding tax
Tax on dividends or other income that is deducted by the payer of the income and paid to the tax authorities wholly on behalf of the recipient. (FRS 16)

working capital
The capital available for conducting the day-to-day operations of an organisation; normally, the excess of current assets over current liabilities.

❖

CHAPTER 10

Organisations and Financial Management

ad valorem (duty)
A duty based on the value of a product or service.

adjusted present value (APV)
Where the capital structure of a company is complex, or expected to vary over time, discounted cash flows may be separated into (i) those which relate to operational items, and (ii) those associated with financing. This treatment enables assessment to be made of the separate features of each area.

Alternative Investment Market (AIM)
A securities market designed primarily for small companies, regulated by the stock exchange but with less demanding rules than apply to the stock exchange official list of companies.

annual percentage rate (APR)
A standardised nominal annual rate of return, used to facilitate interest rate comparisons where different financial instruments may offer interest expressed in different ways (quarterly, over the investment lifetime, annually etc.).

annuity
A fixed periodic payment which continues either for a specified time, or until the occurrence of a specified event. *See* perpetuity.

arbitrage
The simultaneous purchase and sale of a security in different markets, with the aim of making a risk-free profit through the exploitation of any price difference between the markets.

arrangement fees
The costs that are incurred directly in connection with the issue of a capital instrument, i.e. those costs which would not have been incurred if the specific instrument in question had not been issued (FRSSE).

articles of association
The document which, with the memorandum of association, provides the legal constitution of a company.

The articles of association define the rules and regulations governing the management of the affairs of the company, the rights of the members (shareholders), and the duties and powers of the directors.

associated company
An undertaking, not being a subsidiary or joint venture, in which the investing group or company:
♦ has a participating (20 per cent or more) interest; and
♦ exercises a significant influence over its operating and financial policies. (Companies Act).

back-to-back loan
A form of financing whereby money borrowed in one country or currency is covered by lending an equivalent amount in another.

BACS
(Formerly the Bankers Automated Clearing Services). An electronic bulk clearing system generally used by banks and building societies for low-value and/or repetitive items such as standing orders, direct debits and automated credits such as salary payments.

bankruptcy
The legal status of an individual against whom an adjudication order has been made by the court primarily because of inability to meet financial liabilities.

barrier to entry
Any impediment to the free entry of new competitors into a market.

barrier to exit
Any impediment to the exit of existing competitors from a market.

bear market
Securities market experiencing a prolonged widespread decline in prices. *See* bull market.

bearer bond
A negotiable bond (or security) whose ownership is not registered by the issuer, but is presumed to lie with whoever has physical possession of the bond.

best value
Part of the UK Government's plans for modernising local government, embodied in the Local Government Act 1999. Best Value authorities will be required to:
(i) secure continuous improvements in their operations having regard to economy, efficiency and effectiveness;
(ii) assess their performance by reference to national and local performance indicators and standards;
(iii) consult with interested parties in deciding how to fulfil a duty;
(iv) conduct reviews of all of their functions over a five-year period.

beta factor
The measure of the volatility of the return on a share relative to the market. If a share price were to rise or fall at double the market rate, it would have a beta factor of 2.0.

Conversely, if the share price moved at half the market rate, the beta factor would be 0.5.

The beta factor is defined mathematically as a share's covariance with the market portfolio divided by the variance of the market portfolio.

bid–ask spread
The difference between the buying and the selling prices of a traded commodity or a financial instrument. Also known as *bid–offer spread.*

blue chip
A description of an equity or company which is of the highest quality, and in which an investment would be regarded as low risk with regard to both dividend payments and capital values.

bond
A debt instrument, normally offering a fixed rate of interest (coupon) over a fixed period of time, and with a fixed redemption value (par).

bull market
Securities market experiencing prolonged widespread price increases. *See* bear market.

Cadbury Report
Report of the Cadbury Committee (Dec. 1992) on the Financial Aspects of Corporate Governance, set up to consider the following issues in relation to financial reporting and accountability, and to make recommendations on good practice:
(a) the responsibilities of executive and non-executive directors for reviewing and reporting on performance to shareholders and other financially interested parties; and the frequency, clarity and form in which information should be provided;

(b) the case for audit committees of the board, including their composition and role; the principal responsibilities of the auditors and the extent and value of the audit;

(c) the links between shareholders, boards and auditors; and

(d) any other relevant matters.

The report established a Code of Best Practice, and has been influential in the UK and overseas.

See: Corporate Governance Combined Code; Hampel Report.

call

A request made to the holders of partly paid-up share capital for the payment of a predetermined sum due on the share capital, under the terms of the original subscription agreement. Failure on the part of the shareholder to pay a call may result in the forfeiture of the relevant holding of partly paid shares.

call option

Option to buy a specified underlying asset at a specified exercise price on, or before, a specified exercise date. *See* put option.

capital asset pricing model (CAPM)

A theory which predicts that the expected risk premium for an individual stock will be proportional to its beta, such that:

Expected risk premium on a stock = beta × expected risk premium in the market.

Risk premium is defined as the expected incremental return for making a risky investment rather than a safe one.

capital budgeting

The process concerned with decision making with respect to the following issues:

◆ the choice of specific investment projects;

◆ the total amount of capital expenditure to commit;

◆ the method of financing the investment portfolio.

capital instrument

All instruments that are issued by reporting entities as a means of raising finance, including shares, debentures, loans and debt instruments, options and warrants that give the holder the right to subscribe for or obtain capital instruments. In the case of consolidated financial statements the term includes capital instruments issued by subsidiaries except those that are held by another member of the group included in the consolidation (FRS 4).

capital investment appraisal

The application of a set of methodologies (generally based on the discounting of projected cash flows) whose purpose is to give guidance to managers with respect to decisions as to how best to commit long-term investment funds. *See* discounted cash flow.

capital rationing

A restriction on an organisation's ability to invest capital funds, caused by an internal budget ceiling being imposed on such expenditure by management (soft capital rationing), or by external limitations being applied to the company, as when additional borrowed funds cannot be obtained (hard capital rationing).

capital structure

The relative proportions of equity capital and debt capital within a company's balance sheet.

cash management models

Sophisticated cash flow forecasting

models which assist management in determining how to balance the cash needs of an organisation. Cash management models might help in areas such as optimising cash balances, in the management of customer, supplier, investor and company investment needs, in the decision as to invest or buy back shares or in the decision as to the optimum method of financing working capital.

certainty equivalent method

An approach to dealing with risk in a capital budgeting context. It involves expressing risky future cash flows in terms of the certain cash flow which would be considered, by the decision-maker, as their equivalent, i.e. the decision-maker would be indifferent between the risky amount and the (lower) riskless amount considered to be its equivalent.

certificate of deposit

A negotiable instrument which provides evidence of a fixed-term deposit with a bank. Maturity is normally within 90 days, but can be longer.

CHAPS

Clearing House Automated Payment System. A method for the rapid electronic transfer of funds between participating banks on behalf of large commercial customers, where transfers tend to be of significant value.

chartered entity

An organisation formed by the grant of a royal charter (in the UK). The charter authorises the entity to operate and states the powers specifically granted.

collateral

Security, generally given for borrowed funds over the period of a loan.

commercial paper

Unsecured short-term loan note issued by companies, and generally maturing within nine months.

company/corporation

A legal entity, whose life is independent of that of its members.

There are three ways of forming a company or corporation, namely by registration under the Companies Act, by charter, or by Act of Parliament.

company limited by guarantee

A company in which each member undertakes to contribute (to the limit of his guarantee), on a winding-up, towards payment of the liabilities of the company.

No new registrations of this nature may be made.

company limited by shares/joint stock company/limited liability company

A company in which the liability of members for the company's debts is limited to the amount, if any, unpaid on the shares taken up by them. *See* private company; public company.

competitor analysis

The systematic review of all available information (marketing, production, financial, etc.) on the activities of competitors in order to gain a competitive advantage.

conglomerate

An entity comprising a number of dissimilar businesses.

consol

Certain irredeemable UK government stocks carrying fixed coupons. Sometimes used as a general term for an undated or irredeemable bond.

consortium

An association of several entities with a view to carrying out a joint venture. *See* joint venture.

corporate governance

The system by which companies are directed and controlled. Boards of directors are responsible for the governance of their companies. The shareholders' role in governance is to appoint the directors and the auditors and to satisfy themselves that an appropriate governance structure is in place.

The responsibilities of the board include setting the company's strategic aims, providing the leadership to put them into effect, supervising the management of the business and reporting to shareholders on their stewardship. The board's actions are subject to laws, regulations and the shareholders in general meeting. *See* Cadbury Report.

Corporate Governance Combined Code

The successor to the Cadbury Code, established by the Hampel Committee. The code consists of a set of principles of corporate governance and detailed code provisions embracing the work of the Cadbury, Greenbury and Hampel Committees. Section 1 of the code contains the principles and provisions applicable to UK listed companies, while section 2 contains the principles and provisions applicable to institutional shareholders in their relationships with companies.

cost of capital

The minimum acceptable return on an investment, generally computed as a hurdle rate for use in investment appraisal exercises. The computation of the optimal cost of capital can be complex, and many ways of determining this opportunity cost have been suggested.

countertrade

A form of trading activity based on other than an arm's-length goods for cash exchange. Types of countertrade include:

♦ *barter:* the direct exchange of goods and services between two parties without the use of money;

♦ *counterpurchase:* a trading agreement in which the primary contract vendor agrees to make purchases of an agreed percentage of the primary contract value, from the primary contract purchaser, through a linked counterpurchase contract;

♦ *offsets:* a trading agreement in which the purchaser becomes involved in the production process, often acquiring technology supplied by the vendor.

country risk

The risk associated with undertaking transactions with, or holding assets in, a particular country. Sources of risk might be political, economic or regulatory instability affecting overseas taxation, repatriation of profits, nationalisation, currency instability, etc.

coupon

The annual interest payable on a bond, expressed as a percentage of the nominal value.

cum

'With', as in *cum dividend*, where security purchases include rights to the next dividend payment, and *cum rights*, where shares are traded with rights, such as to a scrip issue, attached.

data warehouse

A database in which information is held not for operational purposes, but to assist in analytical tasks such as the identification of new market segments. Data warehouses provide a repository for historical data, collecting, integrating and organising data from unintegrated application systems. The data stored in a data warehouse almost certainly comes from the operational environment, but is always physically separate from it.

debt capacity
The extent to which an entity can support and/or obtain loan finance.

decision support system (DSS)
A computer system whose purpose is to aid managers to make unstructured decisions, where the nature of the problem requiring resolution may be unclear.

deep discount bond
A bond offered at a large discount on the face value of the debt so that a significant proportion of the return to the investor comes by way of a capital gain on redemption, rather than through interest payments.

defined benefit scheme
A pension scheme in which the rules specify the benefits to be paid and the scheme is financed accordingly (FRSSE). Final salary schemes are defined benefit schemes.

defined contribution scheme
A pension scheme in which the benefits are directly determined by the value of contributions paid in respect of each member (FRSSE). Money purchase schemes are defined contribution schemes.

derivative financial instrument
A financial instrument that derives its value from the price or rate of some underlying item. Underlying items include equities, bonds, commodities, interest rates, exchange rates and stock market and other indices (FRS 13).

dilution
A reduction in the earnings and voting power per share caused by an increase or potential increase in the number of shares in issue. For the purpose of calculating diluted earnings per share, the net profit attributable to ordinary shareholders and the weighted average number of shares outstanding should be adjusted for the effects of all dilutive potential ordinary shares.

discount rate/cost of capital (capital investment appraisal)
The percentage used to discount future cash flows generated by a capital project.

discounted cash flow (DCF)
The discounting of the projected net cash flows of a capital project to ascertain its present value. The methods commonly used are:
- yield, or internal rate of return (IRR), in which the calculation determines the return in the form of a percentage;
- net present value (NPV), in which the discount rate is chosen and the present value is expressed as a sum of money;
- discounted payback, in which the discount rate is chosen and the payback is the number of years required to repay the original investment.

See capital investment appraisal.

divestment
Proportional or complete reduction in ownership stake in an organisation.

dividend growth model
A financial model which can be used to value companies based on assumptions about their current and future dividend payments.

documentary credit
An arrangement, used in the finance of international transactions, whereby a bank undertakes to make a payment to a third party on behalf of a customer.

double taxation agreement

An agreement between two countries intended to avoid the double taxation of income which would otherwise be subject to taxation in both.

earn-out arrangement

A procedure whereby owner/managers selling an organisation receive a portion of their consideration linked to the financial performance of the business during a specified period after the sale. The arrangement gives a measure of security to the new owners, who pass some of the financial risk associated with the purchase of a new enterprise to the sellers.

economic value added (EVA)^{TM}

A measure which approximates a company's profit. Traditional financial statements are translated into EVA statements by reversing distortions in operating performance created by accounting rules and by charging operating profit for all of the capital employed. For example, written-off goodwill is capitalised, as are extraordinary losses and the present value of operating leases. Extraordinary gains reduce capital. (Stern Stewart).

economies of scale

Reductions in unit average costs caused by increasing the scale of production.

economies of scope

Reduction in unit average costs caused by the simultaneous production of a number of related products, permitting benefits such as the sharing of joint costs over a larger volume than would otherwise be possible.

efficient markets hypothesis

Hypothesis that the stock market responds immediately to all available information, with the effect that an individual investor cannot, in the long run, expect to obtain greater than average returns from a diversified portfolio of shares. There are three forms:

♦ the *weak form:* A market in which security prices instantaneously reflect all information on past price and volume changes in the market.

♦ the *semi-strong form:* A market in which security prices reflect all publicly available information.

♦ the *strong form:* A market in which security prices reflect instantaneously all information available to investors, whether publicly available or otherwise.

electronic funds transfer

The system used by banking organisations for the movement of funds between accounts and for the provision of services to the customer.

enterprise resource planning

A strategic tool, generally software driven, which attempts to integrate all business processes and to equip enterprises with the capability to integrate and synchronise isolated functions throughout the value chain, thereby creating streamlined processes which can be used to competitive advantage.

entity

An economic unit that has a separate, distinct identity, e.g. an industrial or commercial company, charity, local authority, government agency or fund. (*See* p. 94).

entrapment

Restrictions placed on an organisation due to the limitations of its existing resource base and management competencies, which prevent it from responding to changes in its environment.

environmental impact assessment

A study which considers potential environmental effects during the planning phase before an investment is made or an operation started.

equity instrument

An instrument that evidences an ownership interest in an entity, i.e. a residual interest in the assets of the entity after deducting all of its liabilities.

Equity instrument has a wider meaning than equity shares because it includes some non-equity shares, as well as warrants and options to subscribe for or purchase equity shares in the issuing company (FRS13).

euro

The common currency of the European Union, which came into being on 1 January 1999. Financial transactions and/or financial reporting of member states may now be undertaken in either the functional domestic currencies, or in Euros.

eurobond

A bearer bond, issued in a euro-currency, usually eurodollars.

eurodollars

US dollars deposited with, or borrowed from, a bank outside the USA.

ex

'Without', as in *ex dividend*, where security purchases do not include rights to the next dividend payment, and *ex rights*, where rights attaching to share ownership, such as a scrip issue, are not transferred to a new purchaser.

exchange controls

Restrictions in the convertibility of a currency, generally enforced by central banks on the instruction of national governments

exchange rate

The rate at which a national currency exchanges for other national currencies, being set by the interaction of demand and supply of the various currencies in the foreign exchange market (floating exchange rate), or by government intervention in order to maintain a constant rate of exchange (fixed exchange rate).

◆ *closing rate:* the exchange rate for spot transactions ruling at the balance sheet date, being the mean of the buying and selling rates at the close of business on the day for which the rate is to be ascertained

◆ *forward exchange rate*: an exchange rate set for the exchange of currencies at some future date;

◆ *spot exchange rate*: an exchange rate set for the immediate delivery of a currency;

exercise price

The price at which an option to purchase or to sell shares or other items (*call option* or *put option*) may be exercised.

expected value/payoff

The financial forecast of the outcome of a course of action multiplied by the probability of achieving that outcome. The probability is expressed as a value ranging from 0 to 1.

factoring

The sale of debts to a third party (the factor) at a discount, in return for prompt cash.

A factoring service may be *with recourse*, in which case the supplier takes the risk of the debt not being paid, or *without recourse* when the factor takes the risk. *See* invoice discounting.

finance costs

The difference between the net proceeds of an instrument and the total amount of payments (or other transfers of economic benefits) that the issuer may be required to make in respect of the instrument. Finance costs include:

(a) interest on bank overdrafts and short-term and long-term debts;

(b) amortisation of discounts or premiums relating to debt; and

(c) amortisation of ancillary costs incurred in connection with the arrangement of debt.

(FRS 15)

financial asset

Any asset that is:

(a) cash;

(b) a contractual right to receive cash or another financial asset from another entity;

(c) a contractual right to exchange financial instruments with another entity under conditions that are potentially favourable; or

(d) an equity instrument of another entity.

(FRS 13)

financial control

The control of divisional performance by setting a range of financial targets and the monitoring of actual performance towards these targets.

financial instrument

Any contract that gives rise to both a financial asset of one entity and a financial liability or equity instrument of another entity. Financial instruments include both primary financial instruments – such as bonds, debtors, creditors and shares – and derivative financial instruments whose value derives from the underlying assets.

financial leverage/gearing

The use of debt finance to increase the return on equity by deploying borrowed funds in such a way that the return generated is greater than the cost of servicing the debt. If the reverse is true, and the return on deployed funds is less than the cost of servicing the debt, the effect of gearing is to reduce the return on equity.

financial liability

Any liability that is a contractual obligation:

◆ to deliver cash or another financial asset to another entity; or

◆ to exchange financial instruments with another entity under conditions that are potentially unfavourable.

(FRS 13)

floating rate financial assets and financial liabilities

Financial assets and financial liabilities that attract an interest charge and have their interest rate reset at least once a year. For the purpose of the FRS, financial assets and financial liabilities that have their interest rate reset less frequently than once a year are to be treated as fixed rate financial assets and financial liabilities (FRS 13).

foreign branch

Either a legally constituted enterprise located overseas or a group of assets and liabilities which are accounted for in foreign currency (SSAP 20).

foreign currency translation

The restatement of the foreign currency accounts of overseas subsidiaries and associated companies into the domestic currency of the country in which the group is incorporated, for the purpose of producing consolidated group accounts.

foreign direct investment (FDI)

The establishment of new overseas facilities or the expansion of existing overseas facilities, by an investor. FDI may be *inward* (domestic investment by overseas companies) or *outward* (overseas investment by domestic companies)

forward contract

An agreement to exchange different currencies at a specified future date and at a specified rate. The difference between the specified rate and the spot rate ruling on the date the contract was entered into is the discount or premium on the forward contract (SSAP 20).

free cash flow

Cash flow from operations after deducting interest, tax, dividends and ongoing capital expenditure, but excluding capital expenditure associated with strategic acquisitions and/or disposals.

functional currency

The currency of the primary economic environment in which an entity operates and generates net cash flows (SSAP 13). SSAP 20 uses the term *local currency* for the same term.

fundamental analysis

Analysis of external and internal influences upon the operations of a company with a view to assisting in investment decisions. Information accessed might include fiscal/monetary policy, financial statements, industry trends, competitor analysis etc. *See* technical analysis.

funded scheme

A pension scheme where the future liabilities for benefits are provided for by the accumulation of assets held externally to the employing entity's business (FRSSE).

futures contract

A contract relating to currencies, commodities or shares that obliges the buyer (issuer) to purchase (sell) the specified quantity of the item represented in the contract at a predetermined price at the expiration of the contract.

Unlike forward contracts, which are entered into privately, futures contracts are traded on organised exchanges, carry standard terms and conditions, have specific maturities, and are subject to rules concerning margin requirements.

futures market

An exchange-traded market for the purchase or sale of a standard quantity of an underlying item such as currencies, commodities or shares, for settlement at a future date at an agreed price.

generally accepted accounting practice (GAAP)

A summary of best practice in respect of the form and content of financial statements, the form and content of auditor's reports and best practice and acceptable alternatives in respect of accounting policies and disclosures adopted for the preparation of financial information. GAAP does not have any statutory or regulatory authority in the UK, unlike in a number of other countries where the term is in use, such as the USA, Canada and New Zealand.

group

A parent company and its subsidiary undertakings (Companies Act 1985).

Hampel Report

1998 report of the Hampel Committee (Committee on Corporate

Governance) set up to conduct a review of the Cadbury Code and its implementation:

♦ to keep under review the role of directors recognising the need for board cohesion and the common legal responsibilities of all directors;

♦ to pursue matters arising from the report of the Study Group on Directors' Remuneration chaired by Sir Richard Greenbury;

♦ to address the role of shareholders and auditors in corporate governance issues; and

♦ to deal with any other relevant matters.

The Hampel Committee was responsible for the *Corporate Governance Combined Code*.

hedge
A transaction to reduce or eliminate an exposure to risk.

hire purchase contract
A contract for the hire of an asset that contains a provision giving the hirer an option to acquire legal title to the asset upon the fulfilment of certain conditions stated in the contract (FRSSE).

hurdle rate
A rate of return which a capital investment proposal must achieve if it is to be accepted. Set by reference to the cost of capital, the hurdle rate may be increased above the basic cost of capital to allow for different levels of risk.

inception (of a lease)
The earlier of the time the asset is brought into use and the date from which rentals first accrue (FRSSE).

incremental yield
A measure used in capital investment appraisal where a choice lies between two projects.

A rate of return is calculated for the difference between the cash flows of the projects.

inflation
A general increase in the price level over time. *Hyper-inflation* describes the situation in which the rate at which the price level rises has become extremely high, and possibly out of control.

insolvency
The inability of a debtor to pay debts when they fall due.

interest rate parity theory
A method of predicting foreign exchange rates based on the hypothesis that the difference between the interest rates in two countries should offset the difference between the spot rates and the forward foreign exchange rates over the same period.

interest yield
The annual rate of interest earned on a security, excluding the effect of any increase in price to maturity.

inter-firm comparison
Systematic and detailed comparison of the performance of different companies generally operating in a common industry. Companies participating in such a scheme normally provide standardised, and therefore comparable, information to the scheme administrator, who then distributes to participating members only the information supplied by participants. Normally the information distributed is in the form of ratios, or in a format which prevents the identity of individual scheme members from being identified.

internal rate of return (IRR)
The annual percentage return achieved by a project, at which the

sum of the discounted cash inflows over the life of the project is equal to the sum of the discounted cash outflows.

invoice discounting

The sale of debts to a third party at a discount, in return for prompt cash. The administration is managed in such a way that the debtor is generally unaware of the discounter's involvement, and continues to pay the supplier. *See* factoring.

joint venture

A project undertaken by two or more persons/entities joining together with a view to profit, often in connection with a single operation.

junk bond

A high-yielding bond issued on low-grade security. The issue of junk bonds has most commonly been linked with takeover activity.

lease

A contract between a lessor and a lessee for the hire of a specific asset. The lessor retains ownership of the asset but conveys the right to the use of the asset to the lessee for an agreed period in return for the payment of specified rentals (SSAP 21). There are two kinds of lease, the finance lease and the operating lease.

finance lease

A lease that transfers substantially all the risks and rewards of ownership of an asset to the lessee.

operating lease

A lease other than a finance lease. The lessor retains most of the risk and rewards of ownership.

lease term

The period for which the lessee has contracted to lease the asset and any further terms for which the lessee has the option to continue to lease the asset with or without

further payment, which option it is reasonably certain at the inception of the lease that the lessee will exercise (FRSSE).

liquidation

The winding-up of a company, in which the assets are sold, liabilities settled as far as possible and any remaining cash returned to the members. Liquidation may be voluntary or compulsory.

liquidity

Condition in which assets are held in a cash or near cash form.

London interbank offered rate (LIBOR)

The interest rate at which major banks in London will offer to make Eurocurrency loans to each other, for a given maturity, normally between overnight and five years.

London International Financial Futures and Options Exchange (LIFFE)

The UK's futures and options market.

management buy-out (MBO)

The purchase of a business from its existing owners by members of the management team, generally in association with a financing institution. Where a large proportion of the new finance required to purchase the business is raised by external borrowing, the buy-out is described as *leveraged*.

mark-down

A reduction in the selling price of damaged or slow-selling goods.

mark-up

The addition to the cost of goods or services which results in a selling price. The mark-up may be expressed as a percentage or as an absolute financial amount.

market risk

Risk that cannot be diversified away, also known as *systematic risk*, which is measured by beta. *Non-systematic* or *unsystematic risk* applies to a single investment or class of investments, and can be reduced or eliminated by diversification.

market risk premium

The extra return required from a share to compensate for its risk compared with the average risk of the market.

market value added (MVA)

The difference between a company's market value (derived from the share price), and its economic book value (the amount of capital that shareholders have committed to the firm throughout its existence, including any retained earnings).

memorandum of association

The document which, with the articles of association, provides the legal constitution of a company.

The memorandum states the name and registered office of the company. It also defines its powers and objects and usually states that the liability of its members is limited.

merger

A business combination that results in the creation of a new reporting entity formed from the combining parties, in which the shareholders of the combining entities come together in a partnership for the mutual sharing of the risks and benefits of the combined entity, and in which no party to the combination in substance obtains control over any other, or is otherwise seen to be dominant, whether by virtue of the proportion of its shareholders' rights in the combined entity, the influence of its directors or otherwise (FRS 6).

A demerger take place when the merger process is reversed, and separate entities emerge from the merged body.

money laundering

The action of changing the status of illegally acquired funds.

money market

Short-term wholesale market for securities maturing in one year, such as certificates of deposit, treasury bills and commercial paper.

moral hazard

The risk that the existence of a contract will cause behavioural changes in one or both parties to the contract, as where asset insurance causes less care to be taken over the safeguarding of the assets.

negotiable instrument

A document of title which can be freely traded, such as a bill of exchange or other certificate of debt.

net present value (NPV)

The difference between the sum of the projected discounted cash inflows and outflows attributable to a capital investment or other long-term project.

nominal interest rate

The rate of interest expressed in name.

nominee holding

A shareholding in a company registered in the name of a nominee, instead of that of the owner.

offer for sale

An invitation by a party other than the company itself to apply for shares in a company based on information contained in a prospectus.

option

A right of an option holder to buy or sell a specific asset on predetermined terms on, or before, a future date. *See* call option, put option.

over the counter (OTC) market

A market in which trading takes place directly between licensed dealers, rather than through an auction system as used in most organised exchanges.

over-/undercapitalisation

A surplus or deficiency of permanent capital in relation to the current level of activity of a business.

overtrading

The condition of a business which enters into commitments in excess of its available short-term resources. This can arise even if the company is trading profitably, and is typically caused by financing strains imposed by a lengthy operating cycle or production cycle.

par

The nominal value of a bond, being the price denominated for the purpose of setting the interest rate (coupon) payable.

parent company

A company with one or more subsidiary undertakings.

partnership

The relationship which exists between persons carrying on business in common with a view to profit (Partnership Act 1890).

The liability of the individual partners is unlimited unless the partnership agreement provides for any limitation. The Limited Partnership Act 1907 allows a partnership to contain one or more partners with limited liability so long as there is at least one partner with unlimited liability. A partnership consists of not more than twenty persons, except in certain cases, e.g. practising solicitors, professional accountants and members of the Stock Exchange, where this figure may be exceeded. Other limited partnerships may exist.

payback

The time required for the cash inflows from a capital investment project to equal the cash outflows.

perpetuity

A periodic payment continuing for a limitless period. *See* annuity

Personal Investment Authority (PIA)

A self-regulatory organisation (SRO) responsible for supervising the activities of financial intermediaries selling financial products to individuals.

placing

A method of raising share capital in which there is no public issue of shares, the shares being issued, rather, in a small number of large 'blocks', to persons or institutions who have previously agreed to purchase the shares at a predetermined price.

Porter's five forces

External influences upon the extent of actual and potential competition within any industry which in aggregate determine the ability of firms within that industry to earn a profit. *See* Figure 10.1.

potential ordinary share

A financial instrument or a right that may entitle its holder to ordinary shares. Examples of potential ordinary shares are:

(a) debt or equity instruments, including preference shares, that are convertible into ordinary shares;

(b) share warrants and options;

(c) rights granted under employees' share plans that may entitle employees to receive ordinary shares as part of their remuneration and similar rights granted under other share purchase plans; and

(d) rights to ordinary shares that are contingent upon the satisfaction of certain conditions resulting from contractual arrangements, such as the purchase of a business or other assets, i.e. contingently issuable shares.

(FRS 14)

FIGURE 10.1 PORTER'S FIVE FORCES

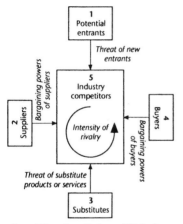

Source: M Porter, *Competitive Strategy*, 1995, Free Press

present value

The cash equivalent now of a sum receivable or payable at a future date. *See* Figure 10.3.

private company

A company which has not been registered as a public company under the Companies Act. The major practical distinction between a private and public company is that the former may not offer its securities to the public.

private finance initiative (PFI)

A policy which is designed to harness private sector management and expertise in the delivery of public services. Under PFI, the public sector does not buy assets, it buys the asset-based services it requires, on contract, from the private sector, the latter having the responsibility for deciding how to supply these services, the investment required to support the services and how to achieve the required standards.

private placement

An issue of shares sold to one or to a limited number of investors, rather than being offered to the market.

profit sharing

The allocation of a proportion of company profit to employees by an issue of shares or other means.

project management

The integration of all aspects of a project, ensuring that the proper knowledge and resources are available when and where needed, and above all to ensure that the expected outcome is produced in a timely, cost-effective manner. The primary function of a project manager is to manage the trade-offs between performance, timeliness and cost.

prospectus

A description of a company's operations, financial background, prospects and the detailed terms and conditions relating to an offer for sale or placing of its shares by notice, circular, advertisement or any form of invitation which offers securities to the public.

public company

A company limited by shares or by guarantee, with a share capital, whose memorandum states that it is public and that it has complied with the registration procedures for such a company. A public company is distinguished from a private company in the following ways:

◆ a minimum issued share capital of £50,000;

◆ public limited company or plc at the end of the name;

◆ public company clause in the memorandum; *and*

◆ freedom to offer securities to the public.

public sector borrowing requirement (PSBR)

The amount of money required by the public sector in addition to that raised through taxation.

purchasing power parity

A theory stating that the exchange rate between two currencies is in equilibrium when the purchasing power of currency is the same in each country. If a basket of goods costs £100 in the UK and $150 for an equivalent in the USA, for equilibrium to exist, the exchange rate would be expected to be £1 = $1.50. If this is were not the case, *arbitrage* would be expected to take place until equilibrium was restored.

put option

Option to sell a specified underlying asset at a specified exercise price on, or before, a specified exercise date. *See* call option.

quasi-subsidiary

A company, trust, partnership or other vehicle that, though not fulfilling the definition of a subsidiary, is directly or indirectly controlled by the reporting entity and gives rise to benefits for that entity that are in substance no different from those that would arise were the vehicle a subsidiary (FRS 5).

real interest rate

Interest rate approximately calculated by subtracting the rate of inflation from the nominal interest rate.

real option

An option based on the right to buy/sell a tangible, rather than a financial, asset.

recourse

A source of redress should a debt be dishonoured at maturity.

redemption

Repayment, this term being most frequently used in connection with preference shares and debentures.

redemption yield

The rate of interest at which the total of the discounted values of any future payments of interest and capital is equal to the current price of a security.

regulated price

A selling price set within guidelines laid down by a regulatory authority, normally governmental.

related parties

Two or more parties are related parties when at any time during the financial period:

(a) one party has direct or indirect control over the other party; or

(b) the parties are subject to common control from the same source; or

(c) one party has significant influence over the financial and operating policies of the other party. Significant influence would occur if that other party is inhibited from pursuing its own separate interests.

For the avoidance of doubt, related parties of the reporting entity include the following:

(i) parent undertakings, subsidiary and fellow subsidiary undertakings;

(ii) associates and joint ventures;

(iii) investors with significant influence and their close families;

(iv) directors of the reporting entity and of its parent undertakings and their close families.

(FRSSE)

residual income
Pretax profits less an imputed interest charge for invested capital. Used to assess divisional performance.

residual value
The net realisable value of an asset at the end of its useful economic life. Residual values are based on prices prevailing at the date of the acquisition (or revaluation) of the asset and do not take account of expected future price changes (FRS 15).

revolving credit
A credit facility which allows the borrower, within an overall credit limit and for a set period, to borrow or repay debt as required.

risk
A condition in which there exists a quantifiable dispersion in the possible outcomes from any activity. Types of risk include:

credit risk
The possibility that a loss may occur from the failure of another party to perform according to the terms of a contract.

currency risk
The possibility of a loss or gain due to future changes in exchange rates.

liquidity risk also known as *funding risk*
The risk that an entity will encounter difficulty in realising assets or otherwise raising funds to meet commitments associated with financial instruments.

risk management
The process of understanding and managing the risks that the organisation is inevitably subject to in attempting to achieve its corporate objectives. For management purposes, risks are usually divided into categories such as operational; financial; legal compliance, information and personnel.

scrip dividend
A dividend paid by the issue of additional company shares, rather than by cash.

Securities and Futures Authority (SFA)
A self-regulatory organisation responsible for supervising the activities of institutions advising on corporate finance activity, or dealing, or facilitating deals, in securities or derivatives.

Securities and Investment Board (SIB)
A private company, limited by guarantee, which, along with the Bank of England, is responsible for regulating the conduct of a wide range of investment activities under the 1986 Financial Services Act. These responsibilities have been delegated to a number of self-regulatory organisations whose effectiveness is monitored by the SIB.

securitisation
The conversion of financial or physical assets into financial instruments which can be traded.

seed money
Equity investment into a new business by venture capitalists in order to finance the period of startup and/or early trading. The provision of the (high-risk) seed money enables the new business to become established, such that it can ultimately raise equity on an established exchange, at which time venture capitalists would expect to realise their holding of shares, in so doing making a significant capital gain

self-regulatory organisations (SRO)s
Professional bodies licensed by the SIB and responsible for policing the range of investment activities

undertaken by their members; for ensuring that compensation is available in cases of negligence or fraud and for ensuring that there is sufficient professional indemnity.

service level agreement
Contract between service provider and customer which specifies in detail the level of service to be provided over the contract period (quality, frequency, flexibility, charges etc) as well as the procedures to implement in the case of default.

shareholder value
Total return to the shareholders in terms of both dividends and share price growth, calculated as the present value of future free cash flows of the business discounted at the weighted average cost of the capital of the business less the market value of its debt.

small and medium-sized enterprise (SME)
Classification of companies which do not exceed two or more of the following criteria in a year (from 1997):

		Small company	Medium-sized company
1	Turnover	£2,800,000	£11,200,000
2	B/S total	£1,400,000	£5,600,000
3	Average no. of employees	50	250

Compliance with the requirements permits exemption from certain of the requirements of the Companies Act and of the accounting standards, and may exempt certain small companies from the requirement to have their accounts audited.

sole trader
A person carrying on business with total legal responsibility for his/her actions, neither in partnership nor as a company.

spot rate
The rate of interest to maturity currently offered on a particular type of security

statutory body
An entity formed by Act of Parliament.

stock exchange
A registered market in securities.

strategic financial management
The identification of the possible strategies capable of maximising an organisation's net present value, the allocation of scarce capital resources among the competing opportunities and the implementation and monitoring of the chosen strategy so as to achieve stated objectives.

strategic investment appraisal
Method of investment appraisal which allows the inclusion of both financial and non-financial factors. Project benefits are appraised in terms of their contribution to the strategies of the organisation, either by their financial contribution or, for non-financial benefits, by the use of index numbers or other means.

subsidiary undertaking
A company for which another (the parent) either:
- ◆ is directly a member of it and controls the composition of its board of directors; or
- ◆ holds or controls, either by itself or in agreement with other shareholders, a majority of the voting rights; or
- ◆ has the right to exercise a dominant influence over it (Companies Act).

swap
An arrangement whereby two organisations contractually agree to exchange payments on different terms, e.g. in different currencies, or one at a fixed rate and the other at a floating rate.

takeover

The acquisition by a company of a controlling interest in the voting share capital of another company, usually achieved by the purchase of a majority of the voting shares.

tax avoidance

The organisation of a taxpayer's affairs so that the minimum tax liability is incurred. Tax avoidance involves making the maximum use of all legal means of minimising liability to taxation.

tax evasion

The minimisation of tax liability by illegal means, such as by the under-declaration of income.

tax shield

A reduction in tax payable due to the use of tax-allowable deductions against taxable income.

technical analysis

The analysis of past movements in the prices of financial instruments, currencies, commodities etc., with a view to, by applying analytical techniques, predicting future price movements. *See* fundamental analysis.

FIGURE 10.2 PORTER'S THREE GENERIC STRATEGIES

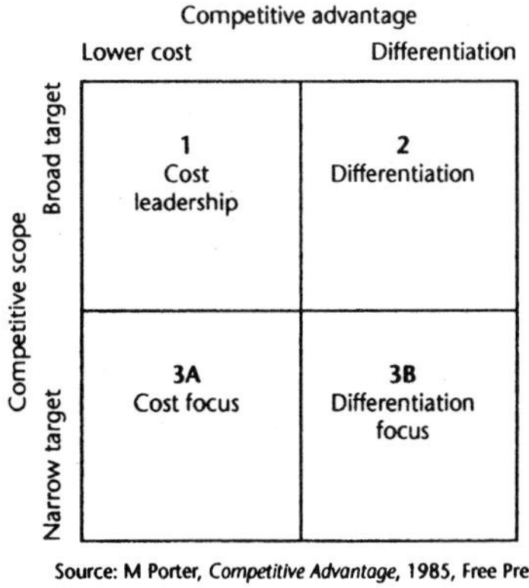

Source: M Porter, *Competitive Advantage*, 1985, Free Press

term (of a capital instrument)

The period from the date of issue of the capital instrument to the date at which it will expire, be redeemed, or be cancelled (FRS 4).

three generic strategies

Strategies of differentiation, focus and overall cost leadership outlined by Porter as offering possible means of outperforming competitors within an industry, and of coping with the five competitive forces. *See* Porter's five forces. *See* Figure 10.2.

total shareholder return

The combined capital gain plus dividend income received by an investor over the investment period.

transaction exposure

The susceptibility of an organisation to the effect of foreign exchange rate changes during the transaction cycle associated with the export/import of goods or services. Transaction exposure is present from the time a price is agreed until the payment has been made/received in the domestic currency.

translation

The process whereby financial data denominated in one currency are expressed in terms of another currency. It includes both the expression of individual transactions in terms of another currency and the expression of a complete set of financial statements prepared in one currency in terms of another currency (FRSSE).

translation exposure

The susceptibility of the balance sheet and income statement to the effect of foreign exchange rate changes.

treasury bill

Government short-term debt, maturing in less than one year, and generally issued at a discount.

uncertainty

The inability to predict the outcome from an activity due to a lack of information about the required input/output relationships or about the environment within which the activity takes place.

useful economic life

The useful economic life of a tangible fixed asset is the period over which the entity expects to derive economic benefit from that asset (FRS 15).

value added tax (VAT)

A tax on consumer expenditure, collected on business transactions and imports. VAT paid by all companies on inputs may be reclaimed or set against output VAT collected.

value-based management

A management team preoccupation with searching for and implementing the activities which will contribute most to increases in shareholder value.

value management

A managerial process which effectively links strategy, measurement and operational processes to the end of creating shareholder value.

venture capital

A specialised form of finance provided for new companies, buy-outs and small growth companies which are perceived as carrying above-average risk.

warrant

An instrument that requires the issuer to issue shares (whether contingently or not) and contains no obligation for the issuer to transfer economic benefits (FRS 4).

weighted average cost of capital

The average cost of the company's finance (equity, debentures, bank loans) weighted according to the proportion each element bears to the total pool of capital. Weighting is usually based on market valuations, current yields and costs after tax.

Illustration

Capital	Market Value	Rate	
Equity	£8,000,000	× 10% =	£800,000
Debt	£4,000,000	× 8.45% =	£338,000
Total	£12,000,000		£1,138,000

Weighted average cost 9.483% (£1.138 million ÷ £12 million)

The weighted average cost of capital is often used:

(a) as the measure to be used as the hurdle rate for investment decisions; and

(b) as the measure to be minimised in order to find the optimal capital structure for the company.

working capital cycle

The period of time which elapses between the point at which cash begins to be expended on the production of a product, and the collection of cash from the purchaser.

write-down

A reduction in the recorded value of an asset to comply with the concept of prudence. The valuation of stock at the lower of cost or net realisable value (SSAP 9) may require the values of some stock to be written down.

yield curve

A diagrammatical representation of the relationship between the yields and the maturities of a similar set of securities. An upwardly sloping yield curve indicates that interest rates increase as security maturities lengthen. This might indicate that investors are averse to the increased uncertainty associated with long-term investment, or that there is an expectation that interest rates will rise in the long term.

Z score

A single figure, produced by a financial model, which combines a number of variables (generally financial statements ratios), whose magnitude is intended to aid the prediction of failure, i.e. a Z score model may predict that a company with a score of 1.8 or less is likely to fail within 12 months. Individual companies are scored against this benchmark.

zero coupon bond

A bond offering no interest payments, all investor return being gained through capital appreciation.

FIGURE 10.3 PRESENT VALUE TABLES

Present value table

Present value of 1, i.e. $(1 + r)^{-n}$ where r = discount rate, n = number of periods until payment.

Periods (n)	Discount rates (r)									
	1%	2%	3%	4%	5%	6%	7%	8%	9%	10%
1	0.990	0.980	0.971	0.962	0.952	0.943	0.935	0.926	0.917	0.909
2	0.980	0.961	0.943	0.925	0.907	0.890	0.873	0.857	0.842	0.826
3	0.971	0.942	0.915	0.889	0.864	0.840	0.816	0.794	0.772	0.751
4	0.961	0.924	0.888	0.855	0.823	0.792	0.763	0.735	0.708	0.683
5	0.951	0.906	0.863	0.822	0.784	0.747	0.713	0.681	0.650	0.621
6	0.942	0.888	0.837	0.790	0.746	0.705	0.666	0.630	0.596	0.564
7	0.933	0.871	0.813	0.760	0.711	0.665	0.623	0.583	0.547	0.513
8	0.923	0.853	0.789	0.731	0.677	0.627	0.582	0.540	0.502	0.467
9	0.914	0.837	0.766	0.703	0.645	0.592	0.544	0.500	0.460	0.424
10	0.905	0.820	0.744	0.676	0.614	0.558	0.508	0.463	0.422	0.386
11	0.896	0.804	0.722	0.650	0.585	0.527	0.475	0.429	0.388	0.350
12	0.887	0.788	0.702	0.625	0.557	0.497	0.444	0.397	0.356	0.319
13	0.879	0.773	0.681	0.601	0.530	0.469	0.415	0.368	0.326	0.290
14	0.870	0.758	0.661	0.577	0.505	0.442	0.388	0.340	0.299	0.263
15	0.861	0.743	0.642	0.555	0.481	0.417	0.362	0.315	0.275	0.239

Cumulative present value of £1

This table shows the present value of £1 per annum. Receivable or payable at the end of each year for n years.

Present (n)	Interest rates (r)									
	1%	2%	3%	4%	5%	6%	7%	8%	9%	10%
1	0.990	0.980	0.971	0.962	0.952	0.943	0.935	0.926	0.917	0.909
2	1.970	1.942	1.913	1.886	1.859	1.833	1.808	1.783	1.759	1.736
3	2.941	2.884	2.829	2.775	2.723	2.673	2.624	2.577	2.531	2.487
4	3.902	3.808	3.717	3.630	3.546	3.465	3.387	3.312	3.240	3.170
5	4.853	4.713	4.580	4.452	4.329	4.212	4.100	3.993	3.890	3.791
6	5.795	5.601	5.417	5.242	5.076	4.917	4.767	4.623	4.486	4.355
7	6.727	6.472	6.230	6.002	5.786	5.582	5.389	5.206	5.033	4.868
8	7.652	7.325	7.020	6.733	6.463	6.210	5.971	5.747	5.535	5.335
9	8.566	8.162	7.786	7.435	7.108	6.802	6.515	6.247	5.995	5.759
10	9.471	8.983	8.530	8.111	7.722	7.360	7.024	6.710	6.418	6.145
11	10.368	9.787	9.253	8.760	8.306	7.887	7.499	7.139	6.805	6.495
12	11.255	10.575	9.954	9.385	8.863	8.384	7.943	7.536	7.161	6.814
13	12.134	11.348	10.635	9.986	9.394	8.853	8.358	7.904	7.487	7.103
14	13.004	12.106	11.296	10.563	9.899	9.295	8.745	8.244	7.786	7.367
15	13.865	12.849	11.938	11.118	10.38	9.712	9.108	8.559	8.061	7.606

❖

Statements of Standard Accounting Practice

SSAP 1
Accounting for associated companies; withdrawn 1997; superseded by FRS 9.

SSAP 2
Disclosure of accounting policies.

SSAP 3
Earnings per share.

SSAP 4
Accounting for government grants.

SSAP 5
Accounting for value added tax.

SSAP 6
Extraordinary items and prior year adjustments; withdrawn 1992; superseded by FRS 3.

SSAP 7
Accounting for changes in the purchasing power of money (Provisional); withdrawn 1978

SSAP 8
The treatment of taxation under the imputation system in the accounts of companies.

SSAP 9
Stocks and long-term contracts.

SSAP 10
Statements of sources and applications of funds; withdrawn 1991; superseded by FRS 1.

SSAP 11
Accounting for deferred tax; withdrawn 1978; superseded by SSAP 15.

SSAP 12
Accounting for depreciation.

SSAP 13
Accounting for research and development.

SSAP 14
Group accounts; withdrawn 1992; superseded by FRS 2.

SSAP 15
Accounting for deferred tax.

SSAP 16
Current cost accounting; withdrawn 1988.

SSAP 17
Accounting for post balance sheet events.

SSAP 18
Accounting for contingencies.

SSAP 19
Accounting for investment properties.

SSAP 20
Foreign currency translation.

SSAP 21
Accounting for leases and hire purchase contracts.

SSAP 22
Accounting for goodwill; withdrawn 1997; superseded by FRS 10.

SSAP 23
Accounting for acquisitions and mergers; withdrawn 1994; superseded by FRS 6.

SSAP 24
Accounting for pension costs.

SSAP 25
Segmental reporting.

❖

Financial Reporting Standards

FRS 1
Cash flow statements.
FRS 2
Accounting for subsidiary under-
takings.
FRS 3
Reporting financial performance.
FRS 4
Capital instruments.
FRS 5
Reporting the substance of transac-
tions.
FRS 6
Acquisitions and mergers.
FRS 7
Fair values in acquisition accounting.
FRS 8
Related party disclosures.
FRS 9
Associates and joint ventures.

FRS 10
Goodwill and intangible assets.
FRS 11
Impairment of fixed assets and
goodwill.
FRS 12
Provisions, contingent liabilities
and contingent assets.
FRS 13
Derivatives and other financial
instruments: disclosures.
FRS 14
Earnings per share.
FRS 15
Measurement of tangible fixed
assets.
FRS 16
Current tax.
FRSSE
Financial Reporting Standard for
Smaller Enterprises.

APPENDIX 3

❖

Abbreviations

ABC
Activity-based costing.
ABM
Activity-based management.
ACCA
Chartered Association of Certified
Accountants.
ACT
Advance corporation tax.
AIM
Alternative investment market.
APB
Auditing Practices Board.
APR
Annual percentage rate.
APV
Adjusted present value.
ASB
Accounting Standards Board.
ASC
Accounting Standards Committee.
BACS
Bankers Automated Clearing
Services.
BSI
British Standards Institution.
CAM–I
Consortium for Advanced Manu-
facturing – International.
CAPM
Capital assets pricing model.
CCA
Current cost accounting.
CHAPS
Clearing House Automated
Payment System.
CIMA
Chartered Institute of Management
Accountants.

CIPFA
Chartered Institute of Public
Finance and Accountancy.
CPA
Certified Public Accountant (USA).
CPP
Current purchasing power.
CVP
Cost-volume-profit (analysis).
DCF
Discounted cash flow.
DPP
Direct product profitability.
DSS
Decision support system.
EOQ
Economic order quantity.
EPS
Earnings per share.
ERP
Enterprise resource planning.
EVA
Economic value added.
FDI
Foreign direct investment.
FIFO
First in, first out.
FMS
Flexible manufacturing system.
FRED
Financial Reporting Exposure Draft.
FRS
Financial Reporting Standard.
FRSSE
Financial Reporting Standard for
Smaller Enterprises.
GAAP
Generally accepted accounting
practice.

IASC
International Accounting Standards Committee.

ICAEW
Institute of Chartered Accountants in England and Wales.

ICAS
Institute of Chartered Accountants of Scotland.

IMAPS
International Management Accounting Practice Statement.

IRR
Internal rate of return.

JIT
Just-in-time.

LIBOR
London interbank offered rate.

LIFFE
London International Financial Futures and Options Exchange.

LIFO
Last in, first out.

MBO
Management buy-out.

MRP I
Material requirements planning.

MRP II
Manufacturing resource planning.

MVA
Market value added.

NPV
Net present value.

NRV
Net realisable value.

OTC
Over the counter.

P/E
Price/earnings (ratio).

PERT
Project evaluation and review technique.

PFI
Private finance initiative.

PIA
Personal Investment Authority.

PSBR
Public sector borrowing requirement.

PSDR
Public sector debt repayment.

R&D
Research and development.

RI
Residual income.

ROCE
Return on capital employed.

ROI
Return on investment.

SAS
Statement of Auditing Standards.

SFA
Securities and Futures Authority.

SIB
Securities and Investment Board.

SME
Small and medium-sized enterprise.

SRO
Self-regulatory organisation.

SSAP
Statement of Standard Accounting Practice.

SWOT
Strengths, weaknesses, opportunities and threats.

TOC
Theory of constraints.

TQM
Total quality management.

UITF
Urgent Issues Task Force.

VAT
Value added tax.

◆
Index

closed loop system 53
code 9
coin analysis 80
collateral 106
commercial paper 106
commitment accounting 9, 26
committed costs 26
commodity contract 92
commodity pricing 9
common cost 26
company 106
  limited by guarantee 106
  limited by shares 106, 117–18
competitive position 43–4
competitive pricing 16
competitive saw 44
competitor analysis 26, 106
compliance audit 7
compound interest 72
concepts 9–11
concurrent engineering *see* simultaneous
  engineering
conglomerate 106
consignment stock 26
consistency concept 9–10
consol 106
consolidation accounting 11
consortium 106
constraint 27
constructive obligation 92
contingency plan 44
contingency theory 11–12
contingent asset 92
contingent liability 92
continuing operations 12
continuous budget *see* rolling budget
continuous operation/process costing 31
contra 12
contract cost 27
contract costing 31
contribution 27
contribution centre 25
contribution per unit of limiting factor
  ratio 72
contribution to sales ratio 72
control 12, 80, 92
  see also cost control; financial control;

internal control; management control
control account 80
control of another entity 92
control in the context of an asset 92
control environment 12
control limits 52
control procedures 12, 93
controllability concept 10
controllable cost 27
conversion cost 27
convertible loan stock 93
convertible share 99
corporate appraisal 44
corporate governance 104–5, 107,
  112–13
Corporate Governance Combined Code
  107
corporate social accounting 12
corporation *see* company
corporation tax 91, 93, 96
cost 12, 33, 41, 58–9, 61
cost account 27
cost accounting 12
cost (at cost) concept 11
cost audit 7
cost behaviour 27
cost of capital 107
  see also discount rate
cost centre 25
cost classification 27
cost of conformance 29
cost control 27
cost driver 27
cost estimation 27
cost management 27
cost of non-conformance 29
cost object *see* cost unit
cost plus pricing 16
cost pool 27
cost of quality 27
cost reduction 29
cost of sales 93
cost table 29
cost unit 29
cost-benefit analysis 27
cost-volume-profit analysis (CVP) 44
costing 21, 29, 31, 38, 55–6

holders' funds 83
recourse 118
recoverable amount 98
recovery 38
  see also overhead absorption rate
redeemable shares 100
redemption 118
redemption yield 118
registered share capital see authorised
  share capital
regulated price 118
regulatory framework 17–18
rejects 38
related parties 118
relevancy concept 10–11
relevant cost/revenues 38
relevant range 54
reliability concept 11
reorder level 38
replacement price 38
research cost
  applied 98–9
  pure or basic 99
reserves 99
residual income 119
residual value 119
resolving credit 119
resource drivers 38
responsibility centre 26
restructuring 99
retention money 99
return on capital employed (ROCE) 77
return on equity 77–8
return on investment (ROI) 78
return on sales see profit margin
returns 71, 77–8, 99
revenue centre 26
revenue expenditure 99
reverse engineering 38
rights issue 99
risk 119
risk management 119
ROCE see return on capital employed
ROI see return on investment
rolling budget 54
rolling forecast 48

safety stock 38
sales 79, 101–2
  order 83
  per employee 78
  variances 59–60
SAS see Statement of Auditing Standards
scrap 39
scrip dividend 119
scrip issue see bonus issue
secured creditors 99
Securities and Futures Authority (SFA)
  119
Securities and Investment Board (SIB)
  119
securitisation 119
seed money 119
segmental reporting 83
selective pricing 17
self-regulatory organisations (SRO)s
  119–20
selling cost 99
semi-variable cost/semi-fixed cost/mixed
  cost 39
sensitivity analysis 48–9
separate valuation 10
service cost centre 26
service level agreement 120
service/function costing 31
services 18
set-up time 40
SFA see Securities and Futures Authority
shadow ACT 99
shadow price 49
share 99–100, 105
  capital 100, 105
  option scheme 100
  premium 100
shared services 39
shareholder value 120
shareholders' funds 100
short-term debtors and creditors 100–1
short-termism 18
SIB see Securities and Investment Board
sight draft 83
simple interest 78
simultaneous engineering 39
sinking fund 101